C000260501

A Life Transformed

Every saint has a past,
Every sinner has a future

Vera J. Quick

**Grosvenor House
Publishing Limited**

This book is published by
Grosvenor House Publishing Ltd
Link House
140 The Broadway, Tolworth, Surrey, KT6 7HT.
www.grosvenorhousepublishing.co.uk

A CIP record for this book
is available from the British Library

ISBN 978-1-83975-735-8

John 16:33

New King James Version

"These things I have spoken to you
that in me you may have peace.
In the world, you will have tribulation;
but be of good cheer,
I have overcome the world."

CONTENTS

INTRODUCTION AND ACKNOWLEDGEMENTS

I dedicate this work to the one, true and living God, Father, Son and Holy Spirit and it is my humble prayer that the words in this book will be a witness to my Heavenly Father and testament to what a transformed life looks like, freedom from guilt and worthlessness, full of joy and peace, the peace that passes all understanding.

Vera (nee Streeter) was born on 11 August 1945 in the Lincolnshire village of Welbourn, the only daughter of Harry and Mabel, having one older and two younger brothers. This work tells of her life's journey from brokenness to wholeness.

Going into a prison as a volunteer is a privilege and security clearance is needed. Security is of paramount importance in the prison system and for that reason I have not named the establishments that I have had the privilege of going into on behalf of Prison Fellowship, Kairos and also being able to be a chaplaincy volunteer for which I was key trained. I have done training and update training, becoming complacent about going into an establishment is a danger. The mantra: "take nothing in, take nothing out".

My thanks and gratitude go to all those who have walked with me through different parts of my journey over the years, your support and help was invaluable. Also to Ian, Ann and Derrick for their time in reading the manuscript and giving me feedback and endorsements.

Last but by no means least, my dear friend Julie who designed the front cover, seeds of hope for scattering on good soil.

Endorsements

Wonderful, wonderful. Vera's life captures a spiritual journey. The record of this journey, told in a child-like way, is immensely vital. Its vitality will challenge each Christian reader to evaluate what it means to be committed to Christ. It poses important questions. How can we process guilt in the light of the Cross? Vera's reluctance, lasting several years, to forgive herself for a failed marriage for far too many years, is an object lesson in embracing God's forgiveness that is available to us all. Her late husband, Ches shines through as a supportive friend and husband, who guided Vera through many difficult and confusing years.

Vera's narrative is a story how church and Christian communities bring faith to life. I knew her and Ches in Brussels. I knew that Holy Trinity was good for her, I had not thought how redemptive it was. Others who were there have also had God filled lives. Thus, the lesson is that this 'organised church' proved foundational for me, Vera and many others. Its spiritual force should not be underestimated.

The joy of this memoir is how Vera has embraced the Spirit of God in her subsequent life. It is diverse, so God filled, so full on. The message for us all, perhaps of our generation which did not accept failure is the need to embrace forgiveness. Psalm 103 is to be embraced. Having said that, this is a narrative of how an individual's suffering, translated by the power of the Holy Spirit, can bring love, inspiration, and a Messianic mind to others in need.

Ian W Jones Professor Management Studies, Emeritus Fellow of Mansfield College, Oxford University and Research Associate of the Centre for Business Research, Cambridge University

Vera has a heart for outreach, from the people who live on her street and in her community, to her work in prisons, the police station, schools and her big adventures in Israel, Vera is always on a mission to reach out and share God's Word .

This disarmingly honest, touching and inspiring work, draws us into the mystery of God's presence in our life. As we follow Vera on this journey, full of adventure, thankfulness, joy and tears, we recognise a woman of infinite courage and enormous energy, whose life is infused by God's ineffable love.

Never stopping to count the cost, Vera is prepared to go where the Spirit leads her.

Ann Taylor, Spiritual Guide and Friend

I just want to say what a wonderfully inspiring read your book is, I have enjoyed it from first to last page and the way you have grown in your relationship with the Lord shines out through every page. Each tear we share with you of joy, sadness or release has brought you, and the reader with you, closer to what it means to walk with our Saviour in obedience and trust. The Rabbis have a saying that a true disciple is one who is covered in the dust of their Rabbi, (they are following so closely). Your book shouts out that you are truly covered in the dust of our Rabbi Jesus and your love for Him and His love for you is clear from every page.

It will be such an encouragement and a blessing to all who read it. Thank you for giving me the honour and privilege of reading it, I have been truly blessed in the process.

Pastor Derrick Simpson

A LIFE TRANSFORMED

"Every saint has a past,
Every sinner has a future"

Part 1

My story is no different from many others who have come to know and love the living God. The purpose in writing is not to dwell on all the damaging things in my life that have caused me and others grief, but to focus on the grace and mercy of God in transforming every situation and experience I have had, bringing healing and wholeness into my life.

(Abuse of one kind or another impacts not just the individual, but those around them, though often it is not recognised and it is certainly not spoken about. This most often occurs within the family or by trusted people known to the family.)

God knew me before I was born just as He told Jeremiah 1:5 *"Before I formed you in the womb I knew you, and before you were born I consecrated you..."*, the vision I had as a child that I didn't understand until many years later alongside other experiences of God's gracious love for me, so undeserved, brought me to tears many times. Being a mother and having my own family, was a great joy to me, but carrying so many burdens from my formative years meant that sadly, my children were also impacted in a way I never understood until I was free myself. By then it was too late.

Whatever burdens we carry from the past, will have an impact on all our relationships. It was only as I looked back that I realised how much my behaviour affected my husband in the early years of our marriage. My lack of self-esteem and deep sense of insecurity meant that I responded to situations often, in very defensive and hurtful ways.

Coming to know God not as someone out there but deep within, pouring so much love into my being it was coming out of the top of my head, so much love I couldn't contain it all. It was the beginning of a long and painful journey towards wholeness and healing.

Formative years

I was brought up in a Christian home, my mother had a beautiful voice and sang in the choir from being a girl, was married in the church and carried all four of us, where we were christened. I and one of my brothers also sang in the choir. My father was in the RAF for 24 years and spent time abroad during the Second World War. He came home to live permanently when I was about seven years old. I loved the village school and being a Church school, we sang a hymn and said prayers every morning, but also the head master said a prayer* at the

---

* "O Lord, support us all the day long of this troublous life, until the shades lengthen and the evening comes, the busy world is hushed, the fever of life is over and our work is done; then Lord, in thy mercy, grant us safe lodging, a holy rest, and peace at the last, through Jesus Christ our Lord. Amen." Cardinal J H Newman

end of the day too. He was a devout Christian man and I had a good grounding in faith. We also walked to the church for a service on Ash Wednesday and Ascension Day.

When the time came to leave primary school and go to secondary school, I did not cope well. I suppose I was a little country bumpkin in a cocooned world and like many people I didn't like change. I found the first term scary and I was fearful even though two girls I had been in primary with were in the same class. I cried many a day as I found I couldn't cope with these "town girls" who seemed very forthright and very different from me.

I became aware that I had a poor opinion of myself and I had lost my self esteem. I was a slow learner and struggled with new ideas and concepts. I was terrified of one or two teachers as well as the Headmistress. The Religious Education we had was something I enjoyed and I found that I had more knowledge than others, which was a comfort to me. I knew the Bible stories from Sunday School. We had separate lessons for the Old and New Testaments, giving us a "double dose" of scripture each week. By the time I was at the end of my school days four years later, I cried because I had to leave. I was 15, had no qualifications, I didn't stay on to do GCEs as I believed I was not good enough to take them. However, I went to college part-time day release and evening classes to learn shorthand, typing and English. I enjoyed my time there and made a friend. Leaving there and moving into employment was relatively comfortable for me.

Rebellious years

My teenage years were turbulent to say the least, my relationship with my mother was pretty explosive at times. My abiding memory of what she said to me was *"you're worse than the three boys put together"*. I couldn't wait to get away from home but sadly, like many other people I made a big mistake. I married a couple of months before I was 21 and 19 months later I returned home. It never really crossed my mind that finding a flat to live in and to leave home would have been a much better option than the path I had chosen. However, what I discovered through living at home for about six weeks and how my parents put themselves out for me, was that for the first time since I was a small child, I understood that they did love me. This was quite a revelation. My mother particularly was vehemently opposed to my marrying and though she never said it to my face, must have wanted to say "I told you so". My father was brilliant and went to see my husband's parents to tell them they had talked to me but that I was adamant that I would not return. I couldn't believe he would do that for me. I'm sure it was embarrassing for him.

A New Beginning

I got a new job in Lincoln and a flat to live in and I remember the end of the first day at work, walking down the road as though I was walking on air. I felt a great sense of freedom, I loved my job and the flat was just the independence I needed. Three and a half years later, I applied for and was accepted to go and work at NATO Headquarters in Brussels, finally arriving there in July

1972. This seemed like a new and exciting world to me; the slight challenge was that I had met someone new, who had asked me to marry him, did not want me to go, but realised that if I didn't, it may surface in the future, so off I went. The following year, he gave up his job, came to live in Brussels and in August 1973 we were married. I loved the European way of life and we made lots of friends who like Chesley my husband had a military background. There were lots of social activities as well as cocktail, and dinner parties to keep us occupied.

It was in Brussels that I returned to church and found it to be the beginning of my eventual journey back to faith and I was aware of God revealing the importance of commitment to Him in the church. When I was 15, I thought I had much better things to do than go to church and I never really gave it another thought. Because I had married in my home church and then found myself in a divorce court, I was full of guilt and shame to the point that even though I was offered the opportunity to remarry in church, I couldn't because of this great sin in my life in dishonouring God. It wasn't until 13 years later through the Christian friends I had in Canada, who told me that God had forgiven me and I had to forgive myself, that I was able to let it go. Holding on to unforgiveness whether or not that be against ourselves or others means we are the ones who are hurt by it, not the other person(s).

We left Brussels at the end of July 1976, having decided not to return to the UK. Ches had gone to work in NATO when I left and he never really enjoyed it. We had a really good lifestyle there and didn't relish the prospect of a three-day working week and other chaos in England at that time. Ches left for Canada at the end of August to find work and a place to live, grateful that someone who worked with his father in King's Lynn, had a sister living in Edmonton and offered him lodgings for that time. Melanie and I arrived in Edmonton at the end of September. However, I would say that after living in Canada, I learned that "the grass is not greener" on the other side.

A New Revelation of God

It was during the years we lived in Canada that I began going to Bible study with these wonderful Christian friends that I began to grow and so looked forward every week to our Wednesday mornings together. Late in 1985 through some evening services in a church, St Timothy's on the other side of the city which were charismatic in nature and quite alien to me, something began to stir within me even though I didn't really know what it was, but I remember clearly the scripture from Hebrews 11:23 "*By faith Moses, when he was born, was hid for three months by his parents....*". It made me cry and I somehow knew that it was connected to my parents. What did it mean? At that moment in time I had no idea. At least four years before this time I knew I could not stay in Canada, I had never settled and the first year there was so difficult, the only way I can explain it is that it "broke my spirit". Winters in Edmonton, Alberta are harsh, we had no car, it was impossible to walk out with Melanie in a buggy and I was pregnant with Christopher. The neighbourhood we lived in was an older area called Bonnie Doon. An elderly lady one side of us was very kind and taught me how to make crab apple jelly since there was an abundance of them at the back of the bungalow in which we lived. The younger people on the other side really didn't like British people! I never really wanted to know why. We did find a church in the area, St Luke's and a couple very kindly came and took us to church, where I met Mildred who became a friend, also pregnant, her son was born five weeks before mine.

When Christopher was six months old, January 1978, we moved to a condominium in Mill Woods, south east of the city. Within a year the Bishop of Edmonton had initiated a mission church in Meyonohk Elementary School (Meyonohk means 'a nice place to be') and we were one of the 12 original families attending. This was a turning point for the better as we fellowshipped with others families and their children after church, generally in their homes. It was during this time that the Bible study began.

In March 1986 during one of our mornings together, I found myself in a heap on the floor crying, I had no idea why. Liz asked me if I wanted to repent and ask forgiveness for my sins, invite Jesus into my heart, which I did and I didn't know that I had so much to cry about for so long. What I experienced was God filling me up with His love, there was so much of it, it was coming out the top of my head, I could not contain it. So began the long road to transformation in my life. Those months from March to June prior to our leaving Canada to return to England were the beginning of change in me and I was brought very low. It seems God had a great deal of work to do in my life. I came to understand that it was obedience that God wanted from me.

We didn't seem to be able to sell our house and on 7 June a month to the day we were due to arrive in England, Ches' father died. He said he'd had a picture of standing over his father's grave and yet, to my shame, I couldn't bring myself to tell him to go. I was fearful of not having any money when we got to England. My friends came and spent a whole afternoon with me, telling me I must let him go and still I cried. When Joy said she would give us the money, I knew that I couldn't take money from her when we did have $1,000 set aside for when we arrived in England. They prayed and I cried until I realised I must 'phone the airline and book a flight for him. When he came home from work, I said what the choice of flights were and he said he wasn't going, to which I replied, you have to because Joy, Liz and Karen prayed and showed me it was right.

He was gone for 10 days and was a great help to his mother in that time. When he arrived back, we'd moved out of the house, I had two cars to sell, the removals company had taken our furniture for shipping and we were staying with our friends who had a great party for us that night. What I didn't know of course, was the fact that his mother had given him £750.00 which at that time was about $1,500. So God gave us back the money I didn't want to let go of and more besides! That was the first thing I learned about obedience. Secondly, the house was still on the market. On the Sunday before we were leaving on the Wednesday 23 June 1986, an offer came in but it would only cover the cost of paying off the mortgage, the legal fees and paying the real estate fees. All we received was six months land taxes back. Thus, we had no equity at all. Many people had said to us, you must be mad going back to the UK as at that time there were three million people unemployed and we were going into the unknown. It was as if God was saying to me, I want you to trust me to provide for your needs.

We left Edmonton on the train, bound for Winnipeg to stay with friends for the weekend, then travelled on to Ottawa to stay with other friends before getting a flight to Montreal and then to Heathrow, arriving on Monday 7 July. We took a train with our eight pieces of luggage to East Malling Station in Kent and a taxi to the house in West Malling, we were renting from a NATO friend Janet, whose parents lived next door. We had arrived to find friendly faces to greet us and food in the fridge

Two days later, Janet's father took Ches into Maidstone to the Job Centre and we were astonished at what happened. He was a skilled mechanic and spoke to a Citroen dealership in Wateringbury just a few miles away. Not only were they interested in seeing him, but came to pick him up to take him there for interview on the Friday. Having accepted the position, Ches then asked if he could take two weeks before starting work as we wanted to go and see the families we hadn't seen for five years and they said yes. We took a train to King's Lynn to see his Mum and then to Grantham to see my parents and others. We bought a car to travel back to Kent, ready for him to start work on Monday 28 July. I was beginning to see how important it is to trust God, for He knows our needs and His provision and timing is perfect. Janet's parents also gave us a cake for Christopher's ninth birthday on 10 July.

When the children started schools in September, I found a job, in a fabric store two days a week in Maidstone for some months. In March 1987, I got a secretarial job, just a 10 minute walk from home, but little did we know that in June that year, we would have to move. This was unsettling for us all but especially for the children to move schools after only one year. We moved to Gillingham in Kent and lived in a specially built complex for people with Muscular Dystrophy who lived on the ground floor with five sets of carers living above. After 18 months it became increasingly difficult for us as a family to remain there. One of the residents told us about friends she had who had a house in Grantham that possibly we could rent. Including the move from Canada, we had four moves in five years. This had a great impact upon the children. When we arrived in Grantham in January 1989, both Melanie and Christopher attended the single sex grammar schools, something alien to them and both found it difficult to make friends, not being in school from the beginning of the academic year. Christopher was very angry with me and when we talked, he said at first (when we came to England) it was an adventure. I asked when it stopped being an adventure and he said when we came to Grantham. Melanie did not voice her displeasure to me until some years later. In my mind I had thought that the most important thing was being together as a family, as we had been in Canada without any family support.

It was a difficult time not least because we were evicted from the house we rented from two young men who decided in October 1990, they could no longer afford the mortgage since interest rates were very high at that time. The Council could not re-house us until the bailiff came to serve notice and I could take it to them. This took about six weeks. The only thing that kept me going was the song *"God will make a way where there seems to be no way" by Don Moen*. With an anxious husband and two teenage children, life was hard. When the bailiff came I went straight to the Council office and the next day, we received a notification of a house close to where we were living. The 10 June 1991 is a day I will never forget as we moved to the place where I still live. I just knew God had given us that house, it became available as an elderly lady had died some weeks previously. I have loved every minute of every day here and still thank God for His provision. Once we had moved in Ches, was fine, but it was then that I fell apart, very mixed emotions and a lot of tears. Today, I call my living room my "Sacred space".

Journey of pain towards Wholeness and Healing

In January 1990, when we'd been living in Grantham a year, I had the opportunity to embark upon a six week Lay Visitor Course put on by the Diocese of Lincoln to be held at the Adult Education Centre in Grantham. During this time we looked at responses to loss and it became apparent that the paragraph headed "I feel no pain" and in particular the words that some people have built up enormous defence mechanisms to avoid their feelings or **people whose parents destroyed all**

emotional security or trust from an early age evoked a great deal of sorrow within me although I didn't understand why. It always made me cry.

Following this course I was able to sign up for a Counselling course through the Clinical Theology Association to be facilitated by a Dr Alastair and Mrs Mary Fraser-Darling in October 1990. This course ran for two years and it began my exploration into what all the pain and sorrow within me was about. The Dynamic Cycle or Ontological Model was Frank Lake's unique contribution in which he took as self evident that normal man is not the 'average' man but Christ Himself as the most normal of men. He goes on to the model of the Dynamic Cycle in the Life of Christ or the Womb of the Spirit.[1]

During that two years looking at the different personality patterns, the sharing, the participation in the triads for listening, observing and responding, fantasy journeys and role play, continued to bring out a depth of sorrow I'd never experienced before and sometimes didn't know what to do about. I knew that is was somehow tied up with my relationship with my mother which had been poor during my teenage years and the one thing that always came to mind was her telling me that *"I was worse than the three boys put together"* (my brothers) and I came to believe it was true.

---

[1] Frank Lake The Dynamic Cycle Introduction to the Model Clinical Theology Association Lingdale Paper 2 Clinical Theology Association

One year I made a conscious decision not to go to see my mother on Mothering Sunday but was riddled with guilt. How could I ever stand up to and break away from what seemed to me to be manipulation of the highest order. A curate in our church at that time was so helpful and helped me see that I was still relating to my mother in terms of the parent and child rather than adult to adult. But how was I to do that? I remember sitting at my sewing machine one day and the words *"I want to hurt you as much as you have hurt me"* came out of my mouth but they came from my heart and not from my head and this just intensified the guilt and pain I felt because she was my mother and I shouldn't feel like that. But I know that I did feel that and it was honest. I desperately wanted my mother to see me as the person I was and not the person she knew when I was an unhappy, haughty and angry teenager. When I asked her whether or not she could see I was a different person she replied that I seemed to be a nicer person than I used to be! I suppose it was meant as a compliment but it didn't feel like it, it felt like she was reinforcing my past.

A vicar from another church in town was also a great help and seemed to be in the right place at the right time. He offered to visit me and I saw him several times. The one occasion I remember most was the Saturday morning when Ches and the children were out and I was distraught and felt I couldn't cope with the pain of whatever it was, like a weight on top of my head and I got on my knees with my arms flung across the bed and cried out to God begging Him to take the pain away. I called Gordon and he came to see me on the Monday. It must have seemed to him that I was going round and round the houses and getting nowhere and of course he could do nothing except listen. Before he left he took my hands and prayed. That evening I told Ches that I felt really strange, it was like Gordon was there and God was there and there was an immense feeling of peace that came over me from the top of my head to the bottom of my feet. This became the pattern of my journey, continuing to search for what it was that I needed releasing from and that releasing taking place bit by bit. It was like I was driven to keep searching and this I did with the help from a number of people along the way be they priests or friends.

In April 1993 I went on a Quiet Day at Edenham Regional House, entitled "Christ, the Son of God", led by Jean Westley, a wonderful Christian woman. We were asked to take a card from the basket on which was a portion of scripture for us to meditate on throughout the day. Mine was headed 'The healing at the Pool' John 5: 1 – 15. When I read it and got to verse five *"now a certain man was there who had an infirmity thirty-eight years"*, it was as though God was saying to me, YOU have had this infirmity for thirty-eight years. I struggled through the day wondering what on earth it meant and after everyone had left I stayed behind to talk to Jean. I must have sobbed in her arms for an hour, it was like an overwhelming sorrow that needed to be released, but what was this 'infirmity' and how would I discover what I needed to know. What did that have to do with *"people whose parents destroyed all emotional security or trust from an early age"*.

Every time things bubbled up from inside me, there were lots of tears and a huge feeling of pain that on occasion was just unbearable.

In November 1995 I went on retreat for the first time to St Francis House, Hemingford Grey (no longer in existence) with Rev'd Andy Hawes from Edenham Regional House and during the weekend looking through books and leaflets in the library, I came across a leaflet from Loyola Hall a Jesuit Spirituality Centre in Rainhill outside Liverpool (also no longer in existence). Well as I looked through it the Inner Child Retreat advertised jumped out at me and I knew that's what I needed to explore. I made enquiries about it, had to write information about why I felt I wanted to do it, ensure that I had support from a priest and friends when I returned and be sure I had support from my family. Having satisfied these criteria, I discussed it with Mark my priest at the time who wanted me to be absolutely aware of what I was getting into in terms of the depth of the retreat which was for 10 days. I'm not sure if he thought I was brave or mad!

On Friday 16 August 1996, Ches took me to the station to get the train to Liverpool and then to Rainhill. I had such a heavy suitcase to carry, there were no taxis and I got a bus so far down the road but still had a way to go to get to Loyola Hall. Someone very kindly picked me up and took me the rest of the way including the long drive to the house.

So began another life changing experience after my experience of renewal in Canada with my friends, when God filled me to overflowing with so much love it was coming out the top of my head.

There were 20 people on the retreat, two being men. On the Friday evening, we were asked to say what kind of instrument we were. I said I felt like a violin that had it strings pulled so tight they were about to snap. I wanted to scream at the top of my voice and cry and cry – something needed to be released.

The mornings were when we worked, the afternoons were free to write our journals; after the evening Eucharist and dinner, we had a time of worship and sharing. This was the pattern for the week.

On Saturday, we had to sing children's songs with actions. For most of us it was incredibly difficult as adults to learn to behave as children. We also drew pictures which had to be done with our non-dominant hand to enable them to be childlike.

On Sunday we had to go out into the grounds and play games either alone or joining in with others and write how the experience felt. Going out to play was fun and I felt accepted but I remember thinking I must try and do better even though I was told I was good at skipping. The feeling was that it was not good enough.

On Monday we looked at the lonely child. This was painful since I had been so lonely for a long time and felt I was unlovable but eventually I discovered that God really loves me but how was I to learn to love myself?

On Tuesday we looked at the angry child. I found it scary when some of the women started kicking cushions around and screaming. How was I to express anger?

There was some clay at one end of the room and so I started beating the clay and it was strange; all the anger was in my arms. That was so therapeutic and then I went outside and ran across the meadow screaming at the top of my voice.

Later that day, I had booked a full body massage with one of the Sisters. It was wonderful, relaxing and I felt very much the presence of God running His fingers through my hair and being loved.

On Wednesday we had to watch a film called "Nobody's Child" and I knew before it came on that I wouldn't like it! Well it opened the floodgates for me, I sobbed and sobbed. I was inconsolable, but Sister Sue stayed with me and through talking to me she unlocked the key and it was just so amazing; something I will never forget as long as I live. She said that I had been grieving the loss of my Mother's love for all those years and that was IT, that was the cause of all my pain at that moment and in an instant it was gone, this blockage within me disappeared and I felt I could take a big breath and fill my lungs with so much air that there had never been room for before. It was a real revelation to discover I felt like I had lost me and never mourned the loss of the love on which my young life was built. I really felt like a child without a care in the world.

I can't remember what we did on Thursday morning, I was just like an excited child, but remember some us went swimming in the afternoon and it was such fun. Everyone said I looked so different, I was and am very different.

On Friday we went on a fantasy journey which was so wonderful. I remember sitting on cushions in a chapel in St John's in the Vale in Cumbria where we had been four years earlier with the youth group. I went outside and sat on a bench with the little blonde haired girl on my knee, who was kicking her legs back and forth furiously and laughing so much that I was breathless. Suddenly, she melted and became part of my inner self, my divine child. My child is so happy, so full of vibrant life, so full of energy. *"Use your energy creatively, just be happy and love"* was what came to me. I am my divine child – truth and love. The divine child at one with me, at peace with me, loving me and being happy to be alive and vibrant within me.

On Saturday evening we had a child's birthday party for me. I said I'd never had a birthday party before so we had jelly, cakes, streamers and played party games. This actually didn't go down very well with the Jesuits as we were just like noisy children.

I wrote in my journal: *"my hope and dream has been realised and I am now free. Having a gift which needs to be shared with others – a capacity to love and be sensitive in a new way"*. And that to continue to grow I need to be able to reach out to people in distress being mindful to take care of myself.

"Once upon a time Vera went on an Inner Child Workshop and she met with her vulnerable child, her frightened and angry child, her happy child and through all these experiences became a free child experiencing healing. Praise you, Lord".

Before we left, we were asked to write two letters, one from our adult self and one from our child and the Sisters posted them back to us three weeks later.

My child wrote:

Dear Vera

I'm so glad you found me. I love you and want to be with you more and more so that we can love and laugh more together. Love from your inner child. V

The adult me wrote:

Dear Vera

It has been so good to meet with you, to laugh with you, to sit you on my knee and cuddle you. You are my divine child, holding all the love God has given me and I pray you will help me share this love with others, being sensitive to their needs, but also being sensitive to my needs, by nurturing those things within when I'm feeling vulnerable, left out and perhaps negative and critical of others and myself. I pray we may continue this journey together growing and becoming more whole as we go. Love Vera

The picture I had taken with me was a school photo and was how I remembered myself to be with very dark hair. What a surprise when I visited Mum and asked if I could look through an album to discover a picture of me as a three year old with the blonde curly hair of the child who had sat on my knee in the fantasy journey. Truly this was from God.

The prayer I wrote on 24 August 1996 before I left to travel home reads:

"Thank you Father that I can bathe in the sunshine of your love, a sunshine which will help to sustain me when darkness descends, as it may, from time to time. I love you Lord".

Down from the Mountain top

As is often the case after such powerful spiritual experiences, there comes the valley or wilderness time and so it was for me too. For two years or so from the end of 1997, I went through an incredibly painful and challenging experience in the church. I spoke out about an event being organised that excluded a certain section of the church, but instead of being able to discuss it,

I found that there was no discussion or negotiation to be had to find a solution or compromise. The priest seemed unable to get the other person to agree to meet. I was accused of other things too, one thing led to another and the upshot of that was that I was ostracised for two years and my friends were afraid to speak to me.

During that time, someone in the church suggested that I go to talk to a Spiritual Guide she knew, whose name I don't remember. She listened patiently as I recalled this sorry story, my thinking she could help in some way. Imagine my shock when she asked me if I would be able to see the other person as a hurting child, as it would help in my being able to forgive her. That would never have entered my mind and was the last thing I wanted to do! However, after some months of praying and wrestling, I was able to see her as a hurting child for whatever reason, just as I had been and forgiveness for her followed, setting me free.

(I never saw her again until seven years later, the day Ches collapsed and died and I and my family were at the hospital to say goodbye and pray. She came up to me, gave me a hug and kept saying "I'm so sorry, I'm so sorry". I wasn't really sure I wanted that hug at that moment and I have no idea what she was saying sorry for; Ches' death or something else. I will never know.)

With the priest's blessing, I went to the church every Wednesday evening to kneel and pray in front of the altar. I read my Bible more and more and God alone sustained me during that time. I was so alone. Eventually, when the priest witnessed for himself, this lady, verbally abusing someone else in front of the altar after church, he intervened and the family left the following week. Two long years on and I was vindicated, but at what cost? It was traumatic.

I saw one of my friends in town one day and asked her if she would like to have coffee with me and she said "oh I would". She shared so much with me. We then had the opportunity as a church to begin to heal the wounds that many were carrying, but by this time our priest had, sadly, decided to move on, leaving us in vacancy for more than a year.

Three of us had been studying Local Ministry for two years and during Lent in vacancy, we organised a Good Friday time of reflection, much as our priest had when he was with us and we weren't sure if anyone would come since we were lay people, but God in His graciousness brought 10 people along to join us and it was such a blessing to us. We wanted to keep our little congregation, many of them elderly, together as much as possible. The one thing I learned from our priest in his time with us was that he taught us to be "can do" people. He was the best priest I ever had.

The Journey Continues

As I reread and reflect on my journey, I am ever more amazed at God's generosity and love for me, that I still find overwhelming at times. I just know that my ministry in the school is exactly right at this time, as well as the prison ministry and after several years of feeling that I had no idea of what God was calling me to and feeling completely rejected and worthless in the eyes of the church, I am so grateful to Zoe Bennett from the Cambridge Theological Federation for the 'cautious green light' she gave me to begin the Pastoral Theology study and Bishop Alastair's initial support. It was quite a journey which had taken me six years to complete and with my dissertation* almost completed, I pray God's blessing on my work and my continued ministry wherever that leads me. My friend Ian gave me invaluable help for which I am very grateful.

(* I was half way through my dissertation, when Ches died on 17 December 2007; that changed our lives forever. He had spent so many hours on his own in front of the television, whilst I was upstairs studying, that I felt I must continue on to complete it.)

I took my dissertation to Cambridge in August 2008, it was moderated later in the year and I got the result in February 2009 just as I returned from my first trip to the Holy Land. I had to ask Christopher to open it, I was afraid it would not be good news. However, having passed, Melanie, Christopher and I went to The Cornhill in Cambridge on 12 November 2009 and I had my "mortar board moment" as I called it. It was bitter sweet since Ches was not with us. Because of my lack of self esteem and insecurity, it took me years to believe that I had actually earned my Master of Arts in Pastoral Theology.

The affirmation God has given me through the opportunities I have had and continue to have since I stepped out in faith and left my Church in October 2005 after 16 years there; came about as a result of a prophecy over my life from Anison Samuel, the Pastor in "Zion Apolostic Ministries in Edmonton" when we were on holiday there. We were only there for five days and the likelihood of his being free to see me was remote . However, he was free and Joy went with me and explained I was her friend from the UK and was looking for direction. He said he didn't want to know anything about my situation as he didn't want to be prejudiced.

Some of the things he said I didn't understand at the time: *"pay attention to the place of higher elevation, I saw abomination on the altar, Joseph suffered to be set apart to be a blessing to his family, God knew the loneliness and I had to go through it to be set apart like Joseph. God had made my heart whole"*. When he said *"your spirit is being smothered"*, I knew I could not allow that to happen. I left the church two weeks after returning home. There are no adjectives to describe how I feel, how much peace I have in my life and I know that my heart is bursting with joy as well as excitement as my journey continues, the knowledge that I need God to give me ever more courage to share the love of Jesus with these young people in school so that in the Pastor's words *"they fall in love with Jesus"*.

I spent six months as a nomad, going every week to a different church and journalling my experiences. What I discovered was that everywhere I went, I met with God and God met with me each week through the Word, the prayers or the message and I left in tears. I was made very welcome and found that after feeling

I did not belong in my own church community, I belonged everywhere. It was a revelation to me. (Appendix 1)

I settled for some months at the Pentecostal church and it was here that I was "loved back to life". Again most weeks I cried, they prayed for me and I began to be made whole again. The worship and the Word were like a tonic to me and I drank it in. I made tentative steps in getting involved though only on a monthly basis for the coffee rota. Something seemed to hold me back from getting more deeply involved. It was when Ches died, I couldn't face going back, unsure I could cope with people being so loving and asking me how I was doing, strange really. A couple of months later I walked into a charismatic evangelical church and 12 years on I am still there. Since Covid, I have moved away from church.

Although I had been part of the Prison Fellowship group going into a prison once a month from 2004, in 2010 when I went to a Christian weekend festival and I listened to a message that I can't really recall, it brought me to tears. I heard very clearly from God, *"I want you to love those men as I love you"*. OK Lord how do I do that? Of course reflecting back to 1986 when He filled me to overflowing with His love I realised that it's not my love I share with them, but God's unconditional, unending love. Since that day, my heart has been in the prison and I do indeed love those men who, in the eyes of society are the lowest of the low. This does include people convicted of sexual or violent offences. My only desire is to listen, to love and to pray. I am reminded of the sheep and the goats in Matthew chapter 25: 36.

Jesus says to the sheep at his right hand: " .....*I was sick and you visited me I was in prison and you came to me*". NKJV (Appendix 2)[2]

During 2009, someone from church spoke to me saying *"it is time to come from off stage to the front of the stage and that there was something that needed releasing"*. At that time, I had no idea what he meant and I would have preferred not to have to go to the front of any stage!

Until that year, there were three of our Prison Fellowship group going into the prison to offer midweek worship once a month, one of our group gave up that ministry, so there were the two of us then and sadly my fellow Christian died in 2012 which left me on my own. Prior to that I was very happy to be part of the trio and hide behind them. I was happy to do intercessions but terrified at having to stand at the lectern and share a word. Now God had taken away all my support and there was no one else offering to join me and so I had to step up to the mark to plan and deliver worship, prayers and a message on my own. I prayed a lot! Eight years on in 2020, I am still on my own, thankfully more confident and brilliantly supported by the chaplaincy and chapel band who are amazing.

St Beuno's Ignatian Spirituality Centre North Wales[3]

In 2011 I went on an eight day silent retreat, this was the third retreat I'd experienced there. The first, in

---

[2] Prison Fellowship www.prisonfellowship.org.uk
[3] St Beuno's Ignatian Spirituality Centre www.beunos.com

2009, was a themed retreat called "Living Life to the Full" and I wanted to find out what that might look like for me as it was 16 months after Ches' death. As we were shown around the place and came to the main chapel, I could feel the emotion rising, I sensed it was steeped in prayer, a holy place indeed. The beauty of the Welsh hills all around this amazing building on a hillside, looking towards the coast one way and towards Snowdonia the other was breathtaking.

The guides leading us were wonderful. Part of that retreat was looking at loss, change and difficulties; the struggle we wrestle with which could be a gift to us where despair could be exposed and hope can come alive, when we can grow. The whole experience brought out a lot of emotion deep within me. When I returned home and reflected on the Jesuits at St Beuno's, I was aware of my need to deepen my spirituality, possibly through an annual retreat there. Only by taking time out completely away from the familiarity of home do I feel I can do this and the reverence to Jesus shown by those people leaves me wanting more. My prayer was *"Lord Jesus thank you so much for your presence deep within and my awareness to want to travel deeper with you"*.

In 2010 the retreat was entitled "Gateway to Presence". We had lots of writings for contemplation, in nature, the parable of the Sower, poems, the walk to Emmaus and most challenging for me expressing myself through movement as I am not comfortable with that especially when others are watching. It would never occur to me that it may be something beautiful in someone else's eyes.

It is to the eight day silent retreat I return now, 12 – 21 July. Much of what is written here is taken from my journal.

It was like coming home and I enjoyed the time of quiet in the chapel, such a place of beauty and peace. Being on the 2nd floor, I can see the tops of the trees swaying almost in slow motion and the tips of the pine trees look like three crosses against the skyline. I pray that as I unwind, I may make good choices in how I spend my time here. It's very easy for me to choose to go walking. I pray for wisdom for my director Evelyn as she guides me through these days. Lord please make it clear to me where my special place will be for me to know your presence and your holiness.

From the texts given to us, the one I felt drawn to was Isaiah 43: 1 – 17, *"I have called you by your name, you are mine."* Evelyn suggesting I stay with that and as I think about how much I love my children, to be aware that God loves me even more than that and at the moment I can't even contemplate that, although this is a truth I need to be soaked in Lord by your Holy Spirit. Thank you Father God.

Following a restful night after the long journey, I began my day in the side chapel and was struck by the sunlight reflecting on the carpet from the stained glass window and initially the red and blue reminded me of Jesus' blood and Mary's robe; the love between a mother and son. As I noticed the other colours, green, yellow, all of them reminded me of Joseph's coat. I also felt at peace in the silence and enveloped by it. *"Lord, I know you are here and that it is a holy space and where I can meet with you, hear you, listen to you".*

I suppose my hour in St Agnes' chapel showed me the busyness of my mind and the need to let it all go before you, to kneel before you, to lie prostrate before you as a way of offering myself to you. Some of the things that came to mind: *"the cry of the human heart is to be loved", "our hearts are restless until they find their rest in you"* and being held in the palm of your hand, all of which led me to the prison, that I and the men need to know these things for ourselves as we open up more to you.

I am so at home in nature and my walk took me along the Offa's Dyke trail, the ferns four feet high on either side of the trail, making it almost obscure and touching my arms as I go by. I so enjoyed just sitting on the fence and then be able to lie down and look up to the sky, so blue, so vast, with trails of cloud here and there. *" I feel so refreshed Lord, thank you."*

The reading in the evening Eucharist was about Moses and the burning bush, a powerful reminder that this place is indeed holy ground and I took off my sandals before receiving the bread and wine. However, I was restless and asked myself what I had to be restless about?

14.7 The next day my journal entry began: *"Lord, I hardly know where to start. You have given us another beautiful day to enjoy and marvel at your Creation. Spending a short time in the side chapel was lovely, the* sunlight once again shedding colours onto the floor. Oh my goodness, by the time I got to see Evelyn, there were tears, tears, oh so many tears. All this stuff about being a nobody was overwhelming, about not being worthy of God's love even though He has showered me with so much of it. When she asked me where this belief came from, I just didn't know. Clearly from what I said, I don't feel loved by my children and I expressed how hard it is to go on loving when it isn't reciprocated – God must feel that many times over. She gave me "The Living Spirit" by Mother Teresa to go through bit by bit. Again I could not stop crying. The jagged edges around the picture of the cross felt like all my pain. Lord, I don't understand, you filled me with so much love and praying through where this loneliness, hurt and rejection came from led me to my mother. I somehow feel that all the other experiences I've had, have just compounded the isolation and pain I've carried. I've never understood the pain of separation from Christopher, that has always been so deep, but

maybe Lord, I'm learning that I have loved my children so deeply in order for them not feel what I felt and that love hurts especially when I feel it is not reciprocated."

"Lord, the Eucharist, as you know, was so distressing for me: "Will you love the 'you' you hide, if I but call your name", the refrain "come to me" all you who labour and are heavy laden and the Deer's Cry on the CD at the end. Lord, having received so much love from you, continual affirmation of how much you love me, it seems that I still need to love myself. I don't know how to do that. I do believe in your love Lord, for I have experienced it but I know that I need you to change me. "Change me on the inside" as one of the songs goes. I know I need to hear in my spirit "I love you for your own sake".

The devotional time seemed to go so quickly and to be able to kneel before you and prostrate myself in reverence before you when most had left seemed so right and then to sing "Worthy O worthy are you Lord", a fitting response before I left.

"Lord, Jesus, you know my heart and that it is full of love for you and truly, truly if you are knocking please, please come in and thirst no more for me, I do not wish to dishonour you in any way."

15.7 *"Thank you Jesus for another bright morning. It was lovely to spend half an hour in the side chapel after breakfast, so quiet, so silent. Job's response in Ch 42 seemed to say something to me about "Things too wonderful for me, which I did not know" and the need* to *"repent in dust and ashes"*. *Sharing with Evelyn what I had written yesterday brought the tears again. "I feel I am where I am now because you have brought this stuff into my consciousness to deal with and that is what I'm trying to do with the help of your Holy Spirit. Please help me"*.

My time in the Rock Chapel was wonderful as was the walk over there. As I read the verses from Ezekiel Ch 36: 25 – 29, I had the sense that the stone in my heart was what needed to be removed as it carried the loneliness, hurt, pain and rejections. In the vision I had, somehow when the picture of the stone changed and came out of my heart, it became a rock so heavy that I needed two hands to hold it. At that very moment **I was set free** and my heart became full of joy and I was able to take a deep breath to fill my lungs, there was no burden any more. However, I decided I would find a rock and then throw it away to symbolise what had just happened in my heart. *"Thank you Jesus for your loving presence bringing release into my heart. Lord, I pray you will show me where I can find this rock. I ask Lord that you continue to help me slow down and to empty my mind in order to hear what you want to say to me. To see the candle burning as your light to me and the great sense of peace in that place with the countless prayers offered there, truly makes it a sacred space."*

To sing before I left that holy place was beautiful.

"Worthy, O worthy are you Lord,
Worthy to be thanked and praised and worshipped
*   and adored (repeat)*

Singing Alleluia, Lamb upon the throne
We worship and adore you, make your glory known
Alleluia, Glory to the King
You're more than a conqueror, You're Lord of
  everything AMEN"

Mark S Kinzer

From the sheet with the statements God uses to describe me as I reread them, it is wonderful to hear things like: Vera, you are my friend, you are chosen and dearly loved by God, you are a citizen of heaven, you are the temple of God, you are a new creation, you belong to God and God belongs to you, you are one who will always be with me and I want to laugh at the idea I am a source of delight to God. Phrases that are difficult for me to believe or accept. The two I have most difficulty with are: Vera, you are a saint and .... in you there is no flaw. I need to ponder on these and Lord I ask you to show me or tell me how I need to change my thinking.

Lord, it was so wonderful to talk to you in the side chapel before the Eucharist. So peaceful, silent and to be alone with you. I don't remember what my prayers were about, but to kneel before you was simply a rich time, just being there was enough. Thank you gracious God. The devotional time gave me the opportunity to sit at your feet and listen to you. Your arms open so wide on the cross and the one candle flickering, whilst the others were still, reminded me of me in all my busyness. This vibrant child also came to mind, so full of energy, laughter and happy to be alive and a joy to be with, not a care in the world. I know that's how you made me to be and as I lay down this burden, this false belief, you will restore me to that for which you intended me to be so I may give and share your amazing love with those at the prison, at the college and anywhere else you lead me.

Lord, I thank you for the quiet time after breakfast in my sacred space with you. The early morning rain has gone and the sun now peeping through the clouds. My time with Evelyn was a much happier one today and she was amused by my saying I need to find a rock! She said there was a lightness about me and I found it easier today. She suggested going to the sea and throwing my rock into it, so that it disappears forever, but I'm not sure I really want to get into the car whilst I'm here. Alternatively, there is a bridge near Trefnant with a stream below.

When I left I felt energised and needed to walk to find a rock. Going down the hill towards the A55 I saw a footpath sign through the trees and decided to follow it. What a wonderful time I had. I saw a small rock in the stream, clambered down to get it, leaving it there to collect on my way back. I found myself in a clearing and walking across a field in the long grass, getting my feet and tracky bottoms very wet, laughing and not caring as I tramped on. I followed the trails and ended up in a corner of a field sitting on a log and enjoying the splendour of creation with God. It was so beautiful. On my way back, I saw some bigger rocks around a tree that I hadn't noticed before, so God gave me my rock which seemed so heavy as I walked back through the trees and up the hill. What fun it will be throwing it away tomorrow. Why tomorrow, well it is the Lord's day and it seems appropriate.

"Lord, thank you for an amazing walk this afternoon, as the rain faded away and the sun shone. Finding the bridge and seeing the water below seems to be right place for my rock. It was so good to chat as we walked together, not much opportunity for you to get a word in! Thank you so much gracious God".

What a beautiful peaceful evening, the sun glistening on the water in the bay and the trees swaying gently in the breeze as well as the birds singing their songs to God. The devotional time so peaceful too and the candle flames still. The flowers a bright array of colours appeared to me as the gold of the crown of glory, the purple for a robe, the red of the blood of the Lamb, the pale pink for the gentleness of Mary and the white satin for the purity of Jesus. *"Thank you Lord for the beauty of the earth and all you give us from it".*

17.7 Father God, I thank you that I decided to lie in this morning, getting up just in time for my meeting with Evelyn. She suggested I go to the art room for a felt tipped pen and write on the rock all the things that had been weighing me down. This could also include the unforgiveness and the bindings to be loosed to set me free. She gave me two scriptures to look at before I set off on my journey to the bridge. John 11: 1-45 but especially 38-44 and John 4: 1-29.

As I set off down the road with the rock in my back pack with all those words written on it, I was aware of the wind blowing through my hair and how I loved that as a girl when I went walking out of the village on a Sunday afternoon after Sunday School – the only time I really recall being free to do that without being questioned. The rain was light and my backpack heavy. I reminded myself as I walked that this was the weight I had carried inside for so many years. As I thought about Jesus and Lazarus, these things came to mind; that Jesus waited and didn't rush over there immediately, thus His timing is perfect, that he wept for Lazarus but that He has wept for me, that He called Lazarus out and He calls me to COME OUT and He orders those around to unbind him and He also says "unbind **her** and set **her** free". How many times Lord have I said I want to be free! And to the woman at the well, He says "whoever drinks of the water I give, will never thirst, it will become a fountain of water (of new life) springing up into everlasting life". Jesus gives me this water that I may thirst no more.

As I walked along I was aware of how heavy my load had been, my shoulders feeling the weight but my back aching too, but also that it had become normal for me to carry the load, I had got used to it over many years.

By the time I reached the bridge it was raining quite heavily and I had to wait a minute or two for cars to pass by before abandoning my cargo. There were two swans on the river bank with 7 cygnets and they dipped into the water coming towards me as I hurled the rock into the water below with an almighty splash; ripples spreading and bubbles rising to the surface. Gone forever! As I walked back past the stream further along, the water was gently meandering between the rocks, not in a hurry, no torrent, just a stream happy to be, creating whirlpools of foam as it found its way.

As I continued my walk back (will I make it in time for lunch) I was aware that I had nothing on my back and I couldn't even feel my backpack. I sang lots of "hallelujahs" from the Hallelujah Chorus and it was wonderful. I give you thanks and praise Lord Jesus, no words can ever express the joy in my heart, the gratitude I feel and the love I have for you. I am excited about the next stage of my journey with you, but just want to rest in you and your love right now and to enjoy being here with you at St Beuno's.

As I continue reading the Psalms how fitting that it should be 116 today. "I love the Lord because He has heard my voice and my supplications ... therefore I will call upon Him as long as I live ... You have delivered my soul from death, my eyes from tears and my feet from falling. I will walk before the Lord in the land of the living ... O Lord, truly I am your servant,... **you have loosed my bonds.**"

Two days later I walked over to the Rock Chapel which gave me a sense of the wonder and awe in the beauty of your Creation and the cows sitting there munching away, not a care in the world, looking at me with those great big eyes. Thank you Jesus to whoever built that most sacred of places, hidden away among the trees on the top of that rock, a holy, holy, place. Sitting there Lord knowing that my heavy load is gone – just disappeared in that rock. When I stopped singing it was almost as if it had spoilt the silence and that the silence was the most important thing there just at that moment. As I read the passage Evelyn gave me, it was as if you affirm me as a fruitful branch of your vine, the pruning you have done in order that I may become more fruitful. Also, that you call me your friend and you have chosen me to "go and bear fruit", it is an awesome thing to be chosen by you. I seek always to do your will in all areas of my life, especially in the community, more so than in the church.

Thank you Jesus, most holy Son of the Father. What a wonderful time this afternoon, enjoying the quiet of my room with the beautiful trees outside and a lovely walk through the grounds, the bridge over the ponds, walkways I've not discovered before, the wooded area and the raised beds. I wandered up the field, following the way markers over the styles, through another wooded area and back out on to the road leading into St Beuno's.

Time to purchase some books and cards, go back to my prayer corner in the side chapel before a wonderful Eucharist with the visiting priest from New Zealand. What a wonderful word he gave about how we 'notice' things especially in our time of retreat. O Lord, and then we got to listen to Ubi Caritas through communion, so special! Thank you again, gracious God. Lord, I do ask your blessing for Melanie and Jonnie in Taizé this week, that there will be moments for themselves from you to touch them deep inside as only you can, through your Holy Spirit.

20.7 Lord Jesus, you gave another beautiful day and as I reflect here in the Woodland chapel on my return to my everyday life, I am reminded that I must not look back as Lot's wife did, that I must look forward and know your Holy Spirit will bless and guide me. I have you beside me every moment of every day and need to remind myself that you walk with me in all things. I thank you, Jesus, my Lord and Saviour.

My last visit with Evelyn was lovely, so different from a week ago. She talked about doing a review daily, looking back over each 24 hours and 'noticing' where were the good God moments to be thankful for; where were the moments that were not so honouring to God, as a way of staying close to Him. The picture she gave me of Jesus laughing is wonderful and I will treasure it, knowing that Jesus laughs with me and enjoys being with me. I know it will make me smile each time I see it.

After my time in the Woodland chapel, I had a wonderfully lazy two hours sitting in the sunshine, on the bench enjoying the scenery and beside the pond with the tiny fish darting back and forth, full of life. One of the most beautiful things I 'noticed' was a tiny orange wild flower with a purple centre it was exquisite, no bigger than my little finger nail. As you care for the lilies of the field Lord, how much more you care for me and I give you thanks and praise. One last prayer time in my sacred space in the side chapel before the Eucharist. Thank you Jesus, Lord of my life.

The devotional time went so quickly again tonight and I found myself wanting to laugh with Jesus, there was no solemnity in me; it was not irreverence but a joy from within. In my head I was singing "My Jesus, my Saviour".

I found the initial coming out of silence quite strange and I would have wanted it to carry on but when I left I drove further south to visit friends for a few days before the long journey back home. I did miss my quiet times during those days and knew I would not get them back until I arrived home.

The 16 August was my Prison Fellowship evening in the prison and I had decided to share my testimony from the retreat with the guys. The service was in the context of communion and Rev'd Jo the Chaplain had asked me to administer the chalice which was such a privilege and to be able to say "the blood of Christ shed for you" with the names of those I knew, was a privilege indeed.

Whilst I was sharing with them, the first and last time without notes, I was unaware that one of the guys had been given a verse for me. At the end of the service, he gave me what he had written down and I was dumbfounded as I had no idea of its significance until then. The idea that these men should pray for me and then give me a Word, was so overwhelming.

He wrote:

"God gave me this verse (Rev 2:17) as you briefly described your vision. I believe the small white stone at the beginning of your vision was a sign of you overcoming the issue of letting go and dealing with the past.

White stones were given to competitors as an indication they were victorious (like a gold medal in Olympics today). Also used by jurors to indicate acquittal/not guilty verdicts in John's time.

Why before the bigger rock? Well God knows end from the beginning, He's the Alpha and Omega and He knew this was the time you would finally have victory over this particular issue!

You have been declared victorious and innocent by Father God. Hallelujah!"

From that time on and still today, I have this joy in my heart and know that God has something for me to do going forward, something I have no awareness of at this time.

New Beginnings, New Adventures

Part 2

As I reflect on that most holy and life changing experience during that retreat, I could never have imagined where God would lead me. There were still more life transforming journeys for me to embark upon and to share with the reader.

That summer my sister in Christ, Joy contacted me and said she and Don were planning a pilgrimage to Israel for 2012 with Break Forth Ministries[4] from Alberta. She didn't actually say *"will you come"*, but she gave me the details and I went on the website, looked at the itinerary and a week later I had booked the "land only" trip and then had only to book my flights. In September she called me to say that they had to cancel as Don had been quite ill and they couldn't be sure he would be fit enough to travel in March.

I was asking myself, did I book that trip because my friends were going or was it something else? As I looked over the itinerary again, I realised that what

---

[4] Arlen and Elsa Salte www.breakforthministries.com

had stirred me was the opportunity to be immersed in the Jordan River and I knew that I must go. I think Joy was relieved that I had not cancelled and I continued with planning.

Arlen and Elsa Salte from Edmonton headed up Break Forth Ministries, and our spiritual guide was Hans Weichbrodt, a pastor in the Swedish Lutheran Church, none of whom I knew, nor would I know any of the people from Canada.

I arrived in Tel Aviv on 7 March in the afternoon, the Canadians having arrived in the morning. This became a significant fact revealed to me after I arrived home and to which I will return. It was a relief to get to the hotel and meet everyone. Elisabeth from Kitimat in northern British Colombia was to be my roommate and she was a delight.

This trip was very different from the first one I had been on in 2009 and it was full of worship each day at different sites we visited, led by Arlen and Elsa, with members of their family and every message from Hans was really in-depth teaching from which I learned a huge amount. We went as far north as Caesarea Philippi; my heart was captured by the Galilee and surrounding hills. One of the enduring memories I have was going into the Church of the Beatitudes, sensing the holiness of the place and as we went down the hillside overlooking the Galilee, Hans shared that this was most likely the place that Jesus taught the disciples the Sermon on the Mount, something we may be able to recite but was completely new to them. Mount Carmel too was a real spiritual experience and as we sang *"These are the days of Elijah"* my legs were tingling and I was aware that I was standing on holy ground.

It was then we journeyed on to the Jordan river at Yardenit and it was encouraging that five other people also decided to go for full immersion too. It was cold and took my breath away and I was baptised by Kelly, a pastor somewhere in British Colombia and Bonnie with whom I had made friends. I wrote in my journal: *"Thank you God that you have washed away my old life and I can now await what it is you want me to move forward with, not looking back any more with the help of your Holy Spirit."*

Because of all the connections Hans had made from the times he had spent studying in Israel, we listened to some amazing speakers in the evenings, Daniel Yahav a Messianic pastor whose father was a Holocaust survivor from Poland, Naim Khoury from Bethlehem a Palestinian Christian and Albert Veksler a Messianic Jew living in Jerusalem who reiterated what other speakers said: *"the Lord brought you here."*

It was an amazing trip to learn about Jesus' teaching, to walk where He may have walked, Holy Communion in the Garden Tomb, anointing at the Pool of Bethesda and to be in the middle of the Galilee in a boat with the engine turned off, a holy silence, everyone with their own thoughts of the stories we know so well of our Lord and Saviour with His followers. The unforgettable experience of immersion in the Jordan river through which I have been and continue to be blessed.

All of the messages Hans shared with the group were recorded and sent to us awhile after returning home. Included was a message given by Jakov Damkani a Messianic believer and evangelist who I had not heard whilst in Israel. As I listened to him something stirred inside me and I knew I wanted to find out more about him. The reason I had no knowledge of this was because the Canadians had arrived in the morning and went to hear him in Hotel Gilgal after lunch. Not one person mentioned this talk during our time in Israel and then I understood that they must have been jet lagged having travelled overnight with little or no sleep, were probably so tired and didn't take on board what Jakov preached.

I contacted Break Forth and asked how to get in touch with Jakov who headed up "Trumpet of Salvation to Israel" based in Jaffa Tel Aviv. I emailed them and they sent me his book "Why Me", [5] his testimony which was inspiring. Three weeks later, I received another email from them saying did I know that Jakov was in England at that moment, with only one more speaking engagement in Leicester? I couldn't believe my eyes and since Leicester is only 30 miles away I went to meet him and listen again. I bought another copy of his book plus some other information about the organisation. I spoke to him afterwards and he said to

---

[5] Why Me? Jakov Damkani Website: www.trumpetofsalvation.com

me *"will you come?"* I said I'll pray about it! As I read his book, I found myself saying to God, *"well I could go for three weeks"*, to which a voice clearly said NO, three months! Really God?!

Trumpet of Salvation to Israel was founded in 1984. The website states that:

> *"We are called to preach the Gospel of Yeshua HaMashiach (Jesus Christ) 'to the Jew first' and also to the Gentiles. The organisation is dedicated to bringing the Jewish Messiah to the Jewish people in a Jewish way in order for God's covenant people to recognise their own Messiah who was promised to their forefathers and long-awaited through many generations but made 'strange' to them through long and tragic interactions with people and churches who were not truly followers of Yeshua. We invite you to get to know us, read our newsletters and testimonies, see our video clips and download some of our teaching .... We hope that you will join us in our calling to bring salvation to the people of God."*

In October, I received an application form from Trumpet of Salvation with detailed information of what was expected of volunteers who choose to go and live in the community house as well as a DVD called "Little Miracles" about the outreach work to Jewish people. There was also information about Messianic Judaism, Questions of Life and To the Jew first. I don't really remember how many times I watched that DVD, nor did I really understand the impact of what I was planning to do. Perhaps that was a good thing!

Having worked my way through this extensive application form, I finally sent it in and waited to hear if I would be accepted to join the mission work. There are many things to be attended to in order to go and stay anywhere for three months, not least additional insurance cover for being away from home for more than 60 days. Having been accepted and completed all that was necessary, with a wonderful friend who would look after the house, water the plants and take in the mail, another friend set up a blog for me for the time I would be away, Melanie took me to board the flight from Luton to Tel Aviv on 1 September 2013 to return on 1 December. The cost of my stay was £2,500.00 which included all accommodation, food and travel throughout the country.

So began the greatest, scariest adventure of my life and to say it was life changing is almost an under-statement. I gave the taxi driver a map of where I needed to be on 19 Yefet Street in Jaffa and arrived on Sunday evening to be welcomed by Gabi, Israel and Marti's 10 year old daughter, they were living and running the house but not home from Bible study just then.

It was at this time that I understood two more of the prophecies Anison had spoken. God showed me that the place of higher elevation was Jerusalem and the abomination on the altar was in the Church of the Holy Sepulchre with all the chandeliers, the ornate pictures and candles which seemed to be a jangle in my head.

The background to the routine of living in the house is very much a family experience, the family being

15/04/2015

people from all over the world who go to help in the work. We had daily devotions every morning before breakfast, teaching two mornings, mainly from the prophets Isaiah, Jeremiah, Ezekiel and Daniel on how to speak to Jewish people on the streets about Messiah. We learned much from Jakov, Israel and Scott who was the pastor at Sacred Assembly at that time from America, the church we attended on Friday evenings. There was a prayer night on Wednesday evenings in a building on Ben Yehuda Street on the 12th floor, affording a wonderful view of the Tel Aviv skyline. There was also a coffee shop on that street called "Dugit" meaning a small fishing boat, where we would go and do outreach. Every second Thursday evening we had a community meal in the courtyard at the house for the congregation and those of us staying there. The worship and the food was wonderful and there was usually a message from Jakov, Scott or Israel. Everyone was assigned a job each week which changed every Tuesday and Thursday was full cleaning day. Israel and others prepared wonderful meals for us, everyone did their own washing. The washing machines were on the roof, and mostly our washing was dry in about an hour. Monday was generally a day off, though I was there for four weeks before that happened. Plans change at a moment's notice which for this organised structured person was challenging but it was good for me, though I did struggle with it.

Gilgal is more than just a hotel! It's a 30 minute walk from Jaffa along the beach path and the place where the teaching took place to prepare us to go out on the streets with rucksacks full of books and tracts. There were two Bible studies a week, Sunday from the Old Testament and Tuesday from the New. It is a house of prayer, a home away from home and a point of unity for believers from around the world who have a desire to study the Bible, be a blessing to Israel and tour the Promised Land.

Yafo House as it was known had been transformed from the early days when people slept in sleeping bags out in the courtyard and by the time I went there were rooms for about 20 people, quite a luxury.

This is what I wrote about my first day:

"It's a beautiful day here and SO hot. I couldn't sleep last night for the heat and I'm told I have the coolest room in the house which is called "Mercy"

so heaven help everyone else. After a quiet morning and a wonderful conversation with Israel who prayed for me, I went out into old Jaffa this afternoon, for a walk along the sea front. It is wonderful to be here again. I wandered back along the little streets with a couple of fish stalls, shoe shops and bazaar type places. The Christian school next door is called "Tabeetha", 150 years old and was set up by a Scots missionary whose tomb is in the cemetery at the back of the house. Also buried there is Thomas Hodgkin who was the philanthropist who researched what we know as Hodgkinson's disease today. I have met some people here from Holland, Douglas from Scotland and a couple of American ladies called into the house this morning."

September was a month full of festivals, Rosh Hashanah – the new year, Sukkot the feast of Tabernacles and of course, Yom Kippur – the Day of Atonement, the most solemn day of the year for Jewish people. There is no traffic on the streets, they fast for 25 hours, they spend time in the synagogues reading from the Torah and for us it ended with a wonderful meal in the kosher restaurant in Hotel Gilgal. I learned so much about Jewish people and culture.

That first week seemed like a whirlwind. With only one morning's teaching, Ivar, a young man from Norway and I were sent out into the streets of Jaffa to speak to people. It was quite terrifying for me and until about four weeks later it continued to be so, until I heard God say to me *"It's not about you it's about me, get on with it!"*

We had an encounter with a young man who wanted to invite us to his father's home to celebrate Rosh Hashanah the next evening. We told Israel about it and he said you should go – oh my – my third day there and Ivar and I were in a taxi to where we had no idea. What a wonderful evening, being welcomed into that family, sharing in the symbolic foods for the New Year. The next evening was a party for Rosh Hashanah for about 40 people; I was helping in the kitchen to de-seed pomegranates to go with the apple and honey in a large bowl. Friday evening was our Shabbat meal, the opportunity to meet more people followed by a wonderful prayer and worship time, Jakov blowing the shofar and preaching, as I discovered, always powerful messages. Saturday – Shabbat, a time to rest and I spent time in the prayer room. I discovered the afternoon was the beach outreach, affording us many conversations where we gave out tracts rather than use the questionnaire. We had tea, coffee, water and cake to give out and the words on the front of the table in Hebrew were from Isaiah 53: 5-6.

I saw from my journal entries that week and the next, I was very emotional and tearful, I think it was so overwhelming for me.

Two weeks after I arrived, we were told to pack some things we were going to Nazareth for the weekend and stayed in a house belonging to an organisation called "Life Agape" outreach to Muslim people in and around the villages of Nazareth. Sammer is an Arab Christian and after some teaching, nine of us piled in the van to go to a village. What happened was astonishing as we drove around and then he said this is the place we are to go to and after he spoke to a man standing outside his home, we were all invited in, not that I understood anything as it was all in Arabic when they spoke to each other. The seven of us were from Norway, Switzerland, Holland, Finland and the UK. It was explained to the family that we love Israel and its people. The hospitality of every Arab family we went to was amazing. We spent the evening there and after the coffee and sweets, they provided us with a wonderful meal. At the end of our time there Sammer prayed for the father, gave them some tracts and then sometime later, that family would be invited to his home where he would share the gospel with them.

I was fortunate to go back to Nazareth a second time in November and again we drove around and found homes to visit, have coffee and speak to the families, the younger members of the families speak English whereas many of the older people do not. This coffee ministry was amazing and the last family we spent time with included an elderly man sitting outside in his pyjamas. His son and daughter-in-law took us up to their home next door and showed us around, just four of us from America, South Africa and me. When we left, Sammer had been inside with the elderly man and when he came out, said he had given his life to Christ. It really was astonishing to experience that kind of outreach in the north, very different from outreach to the Jews.

We always went out two by two and we had some wonderful conversations with many people, giving out Jakov's book and DVD called "The Messenger" in

Hebrew.[6] There are many Russian people living in Tel Aviv. His book "Why Me" had been translated in some 16 languages at that time. Much of the time we had a questionnaire to share with people which gave us insight into how little the secular people understood of their Bible, the Tanakh. Week by week the teaching we had equipped us better for doing outreach and from my journal entries, I see that we did have many positive conversations, inviting those in TLV to join us for Friday evening worship at Sacred Assembly, some people we were able to pray with and many were surprised to hear us say that we love Israel, we love their land and we love the Jewish people and we are sorry for the hardships they have endured over the last 2,000 years. TLV is a secular city and it is much easier to talk to the people there than in Jerusalem, where the orthodox Jews can be quite hostile towards "believers" accusing them of being missionaries and to go home.

Being there for three months gave me an opportunity to experience so much more of the country and the things that stand out in my mind even today was the surprise visit to Ashdod, where we went to a kind of warehouse; foodstuffs and other essential goods are stored in readiness for war. There are a number of these around the country. Israel is always ready for war at a moment's notice. Before the goods are out of date, they are packed into bags and distributed to elderly people, mainly Holocaust survivors living in the area, many of them Polish or Russian. What a privilege to be part of

---

[6] The Messenger DVD, a film by Doran Eran "He washes gangster's feet and sets the prostitutes free

the team filling those bags in readiness to be delivered possibly the next day. How I would have loved to be there the next day to deliver but it wasn't possible.

Gabi and her friend Esther were to be baptised in the Jordan river and I was invited to go with the family, what a joy and privilege that was and I've never seen anyone held under the water for so long as Israel her father did, he must have told her beforehand! Someone who came for just a couple of weeks to the house also wanted to be baptised and one morning at around 6am we walked from the house down to the beach, sang "I have decided to follow Jesus" and prayed for him as he and Scott went out into the Mediterranean for baptism, a holy moment indeed.

Once a year, "Speedo" of swimsuit fame, organise a swim in the Galilee either 1.5 kms or 3 kms and I wanted to do it as a weekly swim at home is my part of my fitness regime. It was amazing, to be with 6,000 others. You are taken to your starting point and off you

go. As I looked at the hills all around, I prayed "*God don't let me ever forget this experience*". When we got back to the finish where everyone was congregating, we could get showered and we were given a bag of things to eat and drink. It was wonderful and as a group from Jafo House we had a picture together with our medals. It was unforgettable, I have always loved the Galilee.

One other experience that was so profound for me, was the opportunity to go onto the Temple Mount, not always easy as the gates may be closed at a moment's notice without explanation, which happened the first time we waited in line for an hour and a half, the gates closed just before we got there. In mid November when there were only three of us in the house and Lior who is a part of the congregation, Scott took us back to Jerusalem early in the morning and we only had to wait about 15 minutes. I had no idea that the Temple Mount was so big and when I stepped out from the stairway, my legs were tingling and I knew I was standing on holy ground. There were all these uniformed men with guns everywhere. You are not allowed to pray up there and sometimes they will follow people, especially the Orthodox Jews. Linda, Martha and I decided we would sing quietly and pray as we walked around. Looking out towards the Mount of Olives to where Jesus will return to enter the East Gate (Golden Gate) was an amazing sight, as well as the Garden of Gethsemane and the Jewish graves.

Many people came and went during the time I was there, some for a couple of weeks others for a month or two. By the end of October Ivar and Lia left and I knew

I would miss them as they were there from the beginning of my time. I also got to know some people from the congregation, wonderful Messianic believers. Elisheva, Jakov's wife knew about my secretarial background and I was able to go to the office and do some admin which was lovely. The one other job for the volunteers was preparing envelopes for the newsletters which go out two or three times a year. We label them and then put the newsletter in and seal them. There were about 6,000 newsletters for volunteers in Germany alone, then all the other countries from where the volunteers come. In addition, we sent birthday cards each month to people who have volunteered in Jafo House over many years.

One final thing to share that had a profound impact upon me happened three weeks prior to my going home. Often on Shabbat, I would go to a local Messianic congregation in Jaffa to experience and be part of their worship. Most of the songs I had learned over time and could sing them in Hebrew and the message was translated via headphones. This particular morning, the pastor had come from Jerusalem although formerly Adonai Roi was his home congregation. I could sense the Holy Spirit around him as he walked around and around the lectern from where he would speak. It was a powerful message and I'll try and capture it as succinctly as I can. The scripture was 1 Corinthians 15: 37-58. He spoke about the process a coffee bean goes through for it to become ready to drink. The grower is most important for the seed to grow, conditions need to be right. We come to Jesus to be changed. He asked: *"Is this just another Shabbat, another worship, another message? If you don't want to change, don't come, if you come just meet friends don't come, meet on a Tuesday. If you do not desire to change, don't come. If it doesn't change you to meet Yeshua and see Him change you, stay at home. God is waiting for you to change. Do we have an expectation for change?"* I couldn't begin to imagine what the congregation felt about his message.

As he spoke, I began to cry and all I could say was *"I say yes, I say yes"* not knowing what that really meant. After the worship ended, I went to speak to Tsachi and explained that I knew God had something for me to do when I got home and I was terrified. I could see the compassion in his eyes and he prayed for me as his sister. I don't remember what he said but what happened was that the terror left me and I never brought it home.

I felt such a sense of belonging in that family, Jaffa seemed like home to me and for about a month after I arrived home, I was really down, I found it hard to adjust to being on my own again and grieving really, the loss of this new family in my life. I had felt God calling me to sell my TV which I did and recalled one of many things I learned from Pastor Scott a most amazing man of God. He said *"what are we filling our minds with, what are we watching, what are we reading or listening to"* if it was not wholesome we should not allow such things to influence our thinking. I've never been a great TV person anyway and I began to think about what I did watch. I can honestly say I've never missed the TV, I have much more time to read and pray and that is a blessing to me. I felt I had so much more to learn about the Old Testament prophets from all we were taught and what we were able to share out on the streets so I bought commentaries to study. I fell in love with Jeremiah, what a call upon his life, to share the same message for 40 years and still the people ignored it, thus being exiled. I also learned a great deal from my study of Ezekiel and Daniel. The greatest lesson I learned from these Messianic believers is that they live every moment of every day for Yeshua, and I didn't.

My son knew I was having a hard time adjusting and said he had never seen me look so happy as when we skyped whilst I was in Israel and perhaps my future didn't lie in a sleepy Lincolnshire town. It was like he was giving me permission to go and live in Israel, but of course that's never possible for non-Jewish people, a visa is only ever for three months unless you have work there, usually time limited. I knew that all I had learned about outreach and the confidence it had given me was for whatever God had planned for me going forward, here at home.

A month on I wrote in my journal: *"I am aware of the spontaneous tears sparked by thoughts of people and places in Israel. I really am missing life in the community house and I'm sure that the churning around going on inside and all the stuff going on in my head is part of the process in coming to know better what I need from you Lord for the talk I will give to the church."*

In the event, my talk didn't happen until March as there was miscommunication and confusion, resulting in it not happening in my church but another. I also had a number of invitations to speak to various groups about my stay in Israel and those were a great blessing to me.

Return to Trumpet of Salvation 2015

When I received information from Break Forth Ministries later in the year for a pilgrimage to the Churches of the Revelation in Turkey, I knew I wanted to go, it was from 1 – 8 May and I also applied to go back to Trumpet of Salvation for two months prior. It was a great joy to get an email from Marti on 31 December asking me to complete the form for "Returning Saints" and saying "your fragrance still lingers". I arrived on 1 March and left on 30 April for the flight to Izmir (Smyrna) via Istanbul.

The next morning, we were out on the beach for the baptism of a Jewish woman who gave her testimony and we sang and prayed for her. It was a special time for her as she walked out into the water, her arms wide open as she laid back fully immersed. Jakov blew the shofar and that's a spine tingling experience. For many of the Jewish people who give their lives to Christ, the cost is great and so it was for her. Her husband and children rejected her and although she experienced the love and saving grace of God, she was alone, having to find work and a place to live. It was a great joy to speak to her and pray with her at our Shabbat worship. I met other young people who had similarly experienced rejection from their families who couldn't accept their becoming believers in Yeshua HaMaschiah. Scott had returned to America since my previous visit and Baruch a Jewish believer from

South Africa was the pastor, a very different person but I learned a lot from him too.

There was much more teaching and outreach, some of the highlights of my time being the festival of Purim which was performed at our celebration meal. We were all required to dress up for the occasion and I got a mask with feathers and lights. I will never ever read the story of Esther in the same light ever again as people acted out the story of Esther and Mordecai. It was so funny, some of the costumes were brilliant, the sceptre on this occasion a wooden spoon. To see Yonathan, Marti's eldest son playing the part of Haman was priceless. Was he enjoying being wicked?

Being there for Passover (Pesach) was a special experience especially as the next day was Resurrection Day. What I found most powerful and really emotional was the thought that *"here I am just an hour away from Jerusalem where Jesus was crucified, how the sky turned black, and because of His amazing sacrifice for me and the whole world, I have life and life in abundance but more importantly eternal life"*.

Sunday is a working day and I wondered how I might feel about not going to "church" on Easter Day as we were going to do outreach in TLV close to Rabin Square. We had some wonderful conversations along the street and the moments when no one was walking by I was singing "Sing Hallelujah to the Lord", the verses – "Jesus is risen from the dead and Jesus is coming back again." So my Resurrection worship was out on the street.

Holocaust Memorial Day was a very solemn occasion and in the evening in Hotel Gilgal six large candles were lit with a short ceremony, one for each million Jews slaughtered, the eve of Yom HaShoah. Coffee shops and other places of leisure were closed at 8pm. At 10 am the next morning a siren sounded for one minute across all Israel. People driving, stopped, stepped out of their vehicles to stand in silence along with those on the pavements, a very poignant moment for me as well as the people of Israel.

Doing outreach in Jerusalem is challenging, something I had not done before and at first my courage failed me, I felt inadequate and insecure, but I prayed and asked the Holy Spirit to cover my weakness and insecurity; that made such a difference and Jill and I had some good conversations as well as those not so with Orthodox Jews. I shared with Ziv afterwards how I had felt and was encouraged by his response, that he always feels the spirit of unbelief or heaviness every time he goes there.

The other place I visited that had a great impact on me was the Women's Centre called Aviv. It's open two days a week and offers prostitutes and drug addicted women a sanctuary to go and have a shower, a meal provided by Hotel Gilgal on Mondays and Thursdays; there are clothes available for them to have and they have scripture read to them. They can also sleep whilst there and sometimes someone is there to give them a massage. I needed to go back there to overcome my fear of seeing these young women in such a bad place. Occasionally, a young woman has accepted Jesus and had the opportunity to go to a rehabilitation place in

Jerusalem for a year. I asked the women in charge if many are able to turn their lives around and the response was *"no not really, we love them until they die"*. I found it heartbreaking.

The last beach outreach in my time there was wonderful, I so enjoyed it and gone was the fear that gripped me during my first trip; aware that I was confident in speaking to those walking along the beach path. So many people out there to chat with and give books to, a young man Amil who was going to read the book on his way back to Haifa, an elderly couple from the Ukraine who thanked us for our prayers for their country and a mother and son who were so open. I shared my testimony with him of what God had done in my life and I had never been asked before *"how can I have what you have?"* Being able to say *"you need to repent, and invite Yeshua into your heart"* was wonderful. When they've read the book they will invite Baruch and Karen to visit them at home to talk. It was so exciting, we were out for three and a half hours – no wonder my back was aching when I got home.

Just a few days left before I left for Turkey, Ziv took us to Jericho, the Jordan river closest to the place Jesus would have been baptised, the Mount of Temptation with stunning views over Jericho where Jesus was tempted and the spring purified by Elisha and then on to the Dead Sea; the Judean desert hills have a beauty all their own.

I was asked to write up a testimony of my time there for the Trumpet newsletter.

"As I reflect on my time in Jafo House over the past two months, it has been such a rich and rewarding time as well as personally challenging. God always has something new to teach me about myself! Being here as part of the community is different from coming to take part in a specific summer campaign.

The teaching I have experienced from Jakov, Israel, Baruch and Ziv prepared us to go out two by two on the streets of Jaffa-Tel Aviv to talk to the Jewish people, giving us understanding of the context in which they live. Most people we talk to marvel that we come from many parts of the world to say that we love them, pray for them and love the land of Israel. They seem surprised that we know anything about "their" Bible with the prophecies, the truth about Yeshua and that this truth is for them too. Being part of this family of God in community makes it hard to leave, the Bible studies, the teaching, worship with the congregation and the friendships made remain in my heart, part of which will stay here..... until the next time?"

The pilgrimage to the Churches of the Revelation was like a whirlwind and after a few days, one set of ruins look much like another. Having said that, it brought to life for me the chapters about the seven churches at the beginning of the book of Revelation. I have pages of notes from the teaching at every site. Several times as we worshipped and prayed among the ruins, I knew I was standing on holy ground. The highlight of the whole journey for me, was the boat trip over to Patmos Island where John was banished by the cruel Emperor Domitian, because he would not worship him as a god and after he died all records of him were erased; he murdered his mother. The next emperor Trajan had allowed John to return to Ephesus where he died.

The four hour ferry journey to Patmos was wonderful and we enjoyed some worship out on deck in the sunshine with a message from Hans from Acts 27, reminding us of Paul's eventful journey to Rome.

Patmos was bigger than I had expected and the population is around 3,100. After leaving our bags at the hotel, we went to the cave of the Apocalypse where John had the vision we read of in the book of Revelation. I was shocked to find that the simplicity of the cave as it would have been when John was there no longer existed. It was full of icons, lamps, pictures, all kinds of things that for me, did not belong in that holy place.

The monastery, a prominent landmark on the top of the hill with a spectacular view over the island run by the Greek Orthodox Church had stems of lavender scattered throughout the building and courtyard as it was St John's day for them. We heard the bells ringing too. The next morning we travelled to another part of the island to see a tiny church, room enough for only 12 people inside and we sang "He is Lord" in and around it. It was incredibly emotional being there and I wasn't the only one in tears. From there we travelled to another part of the island to have communion on the beach. It was a holy time, an opportunity to confess our sins in a silent moment and as we went to receive, we were asked to put the stones we had collected from the beach, on the wall to make an altar which looked like a cairn. As I looked at the one I had picked up I noticed it was the shape of the Galilee and that really touched my heart.

The following give us prophetic insight into the highest promise to the coldest church:

Ephesus, was promised to eat from the tree of life
Smyrna, to be given the crown of life
Pergamos (Pergamum) hidden manna and a stone
    with a new name
Thyatira, to rule over nations and receive the
    morning star
Sardis, to be clothed in white
Philadelphia, a place in God's presence, a new name
    and the New Jerusalem
Laodicea, to share Christ's throne and sit with Him

Final visit to Trumpet of Salvation and Israel 2016

Once again, I joined Break Forth Ministries for a tour. I was looking forward to going to some sites I'd not been to before including the Ramon Crater in the desert, Eilat and a site in Mukavir, Jordan where John the Baptist was beheaded. The border crossing from Jordan back to Israel took about three hours as it was Shabbat and very few staff available to check our documentation. However, Hans had been in contact with Tass Abu Saada in Jericho who headed up Seeds of Hope ministry;[7] an astonishing story of God's hand upon his life. We were able to have lunch in his restaurant there and listened to him. He

---

[7] Seeds of Hope Ministry in Jericho and Jerusalem

wrote a book called "Once an Arafat Man"[8] in which he tells of being turned from a trained marksman, killing many people to a spirit filled Christian working to bring humanitarian aid and education from pre-schoolers to kindergarten into the lives of Arab families. There was also a school in Jerusalem where Jewish and Arab children are together and learning love and respect for one another rather than hatred. He was born in Gaza in 1951. I read the book when I returned home as well as "The Mind of Terror". That visit in Jericho was definitely not on the itinerary.

I returned to Yafo House on 16 May to do more outreach but also to join one of the summer campaigns, something I had not done before as I wasn't sure if the days would be too long for me. Israel gave me a hug and said *"why you not stay three months?"* The first morning devotional was led by Ziv, who lived in the house and was studying to become a tour guide in Israel. He came from the north and was the only believer in his family. He shared that God had brought a shaking into the congregation since the previous year and how necessary it was because of comfort and complacency. I wrote in my blog *"I'm not sure I know what comfortable is any more as God continues to stretch me beyond what I feel I can be and do. I simply have to trust and be obedient."*

After three quiet days, the house was buzzing with so many new arrivals and our community meal for 30+

[8] Tass Abu Saada Books: "Once an Arafat Man" ISBN 978-1-4143-3444-8 and "The Mind of Terror" ISBN 978-1-4964-1187-7

people; truly international. More young people had arrived from Finland, Alex from South Africa, Josephina from Holland and Anny from Denmark, a group from America leaving the next day.

Anny and I walked back from the hotel after the teaching and gave out some leaflets and also had a conversation with a Holocaust survivor telling a familiar story about not believing in God because of his experiences, but he took Jakov's book in Hebrew for his children. I notice I had written in my blog *"it was good to get out there to do some outreach, Lord, I pray you will use me to sow good seed in good soil, trusting you to produce the harvest"* a far cry from 2013!

A week or so later a film crew invaded the house in the afternoon, going on to the roof and then into the cemetery behind the garden; they finally finished at 9pm. This I discovered, was for Jakov's new film "A New Spirit",[9] to which I will return.

Yaron, another Jewish believer, who cooked quite a lot of meals for us invited us to go with him to the "bus station" area where many lost souls inhabit the streets. It was an amazing morning and he goes there every Friday to show love and compassion for these people. We gave out apples, chocolate bars and water to the homeless men and prostitutes in the area. It was so humbling to talk to them, to pray with them and to give them encouragement. A couple of weeks later Yaron

---

[9] A New Spirit DVD, a drama by Doran Eran inspired by the best-selling autobiography of Jakov Damkani

gave me the opportunity to do street ministry again and it was the best day I'd had all week. I just came alive out there as we gave out the goodies; praying for them even if they didn't understand what I said. The men's centre offers a meal on Fridays and was busy. As I looked at the eyes of one of the guys, they were so sad and again I touched his shoulder and prayed for him.

I do have great compassion for homeless people, most of them were men, who I met regularly at home on Saturday evenings when we were out street pastoring in the town centre late at night. We always bought food for them and took hot chocolate in a flask for those cold winter nights. I often wondered what had happened in

their lives for them to find themselves on the streets. For some, it would have been release from prison with nowhere to stay.

Back to "A New Spirit" oh my, we were asked to be extras for some parts of the film. The film director said to us that by the end of the day, we would never want to be actors and he was certainly right about that! We left home at 6am in the morning arriving back home about 4pm. The following day we were in a different location, filming the part where Jakov (an actor playing the young Jakov) was being welcomed into a Christian community. It was hot and the scenes long – repeated endlessly. We had been warned. Lunch was around 3pm and then Jakov's baptism was filmed. It was a really moving scene. Three years later, Elisheva sent me a copy of the finished film, oh my goodness I didn't expect to see myself with my arms high in the air praising God as

Jakov was welcomed into the Christian community. I secretly hoped that any bits filmed of me would be on the cutting room floor.

It was an exhausting two days, but the next day Ziv took nine of us to the beach at Caesarea. I had a lovely swim and then sat in the shallow water to pray. I was so emotional, many tears as I was overwhelmed by God's mercy and generosity to me, just being there. The guys were playing Frisbee for awhile and then set up the net for us to play beach volleyball. I've never played volleyball in my life before but we had such fun and after awhile I even managed to hit the ball hard enough to get it over the net to the other side, but not before Ziv suggested I serve from way inside the line! Before we left, Andreas saw some soldiers further up the beach, so we took the books we had and went to talk to them. They were all female, one wanted a hug and they thanked us for our love and prayers for what they do and they took all the books and "The Messenger" DVD.

The following weekend I went with Israel, Ziv, Andreas and Alex to Kiryat Sh'mona about two and a half hours north of TLV. We went to spend a couple of nights in the apartment there to fellowship with the congregation and have Bible study too. This is the place where Jakov was born and it has a population of about 24,000 people. The view from the living room is Mount Hermon in the distance.

Age is no barrier when you're with these young people and Ziv took Alex, Andreas, Katya and I to the river to swim, another first for me; it was so refreshing and not as cold as I thought it might be. When Ziv said we were going to swim in another river the next day I imagined it to be similar but it was a long way down and when we got to the bottom it was clear to me that I couldn't swim in this fast running, clear COLD water coming down from the mountain. I managed to get up to my shoulders whilst Andreas was already face down in the water and telling me how refreshing it was! As I reflected on this white water rushing by, I thought of the verse in Revelation 22:1 *"And he showed me a pure river of the water of life, clear as crystal, proceeding from the throne of God and the Lamb"*. It really was clear as crystal.

Ziv put the watermelon in the water to cool and an hour later we were sitting on the rocks eating watermelon. He gave me a huge piece and said I needed to get my face in it and eat Israeli style. He laughed when I dipped my hands in the water to clean my face from all the juice that had run down my chin. Having got almost dry sitting on the rocks, it was time to negotiate the water and more rocks to get back to the other side where our clothes were but I slipped and got wetter than hoped. Alex telling me to reach out for his hand, that was a bit scary. I wasn't the only one tired when we got home. However, I lived to tell the tale. The evening was fellowship and Bible study with Scott and the congregation. Afterwards we had great food and fellowship.

The next day we did some outreach in Kiryat Sh'mona after Ziv had taken us to see the memorial to a man called Trumpeldor who with others in 1920 fought with the Bedouins to claim land, 28 years before Israel became a nation state. On another memorial was written *"In blood and fire we fell and in blood and fire we shall rise"*, quite prophetic really. Kiryat Sh'mona is about 4 kms from the Lebanese border.

We left to go home the next day and two couples from the USA and eight people from Norway came to Bible study that evening. Another volunteer from America, Anthony arrived to spend three months in the house. Israel led our devotions in the morning, moving on more or less from where he left off from Bible study, talking about spiritual wisdom, the only wisdom that counts. I feel this is something that will challenge me when I go home. *"How will I live in such a way that there will be no mistaking that I am consumed with the things of God?"*

Sunday 12 June was Shavuot (Pentecost) and we went to Yad HaShemona, a little south of Jerusalem. I was given to understand that this is the only Messianic Kibbutzim in Israel. There was a huge picnic there to celebrate the Feast of Weeks found in Leviticus 23: 15-22. There was a lovely atmosphere, people making garlands of flowers for their hair, worship and many crafts and books for sale. We left after our picnic and went into the Old City, first to Christchurch to pray then to wander the streets and to the Upper Room where we shared bread and juice together reminding us of Jesus' Last Supper with the disciples.

Back to Yafo House to prepare the rooms for the ten people who would be joining the campaign on Friday.

This was the one thing I hadn't participated in before and Israel wasn't sure it would go ahead with so few people. Normally, it is large undertaking using a coach to take the volunteers all over the country to do outreach, singing and dancing and flag waving through the streets, giving out brochures, books and other materials. We wore orange tee shirts that say *"Your people shall be my people and your God my God"* from the book of Ruth, in Hebrew on the front and English on the back. My room- mate arrived at 1 am in the morning, Christina from Dallas, Texas. We were an international group from France, Holland, New Zealand, America, Northern Ireland and me flying the flag for England.

We had some intensive teaching with Jakov as a group on Shabbat, before beach outreach in the afternoon and the next morning we had devotions at 7.30am, breakfast at the hotel, more teaching for the questionnaire we were to use, packed ourselves lunch; one group went to Ramat Gan and we went to Holon. When we came back together, everyone had stories to tell of great encounters. We travelled north to Caesarea, met up with the other group, had our picnic lunches and then a tour of the whole site with Ziv as our guide. It's such an important place in biblical history: Peter called to go to see Cornelius, who became the first Gentile believer, Paul under house arrest there for 18 months though he had quite a bit of freedom, until he insisted on going to Rome. The history of Herod who built this great port city is amazing, just ruins now having been conquered by different groups throughout the ages. We met and prayed for three army guys and a couple who had just got married. Back to Jaffa for dinner, an early night ready for devotions again at 7.30am, packed to go to Jerusalem for an overnight stay in a kibbutzim.

Outreach in Ben Yehuda Street in Jerusalem was challenging, we being very identifiable with our flags, orange tee shirts and singing. When the Orthodox Jews caught up with us, they started shouting and following us. They tried to take the tracts from us. Two of them were young just teenagers. We carried on singing, the louder we sang the more they shouted. One man on a cycle tried to weave in and out of us to break us up. Israel spoke to them and we tried to say to them that we love them and the Land but they would not listen. Bystanders watching, were supporting us. They followed us until we got into the Old City and Christchurch where they left. It reminded me of the scripture

"O Jerusalem, Jerusalem, the one who kills the prophets and stones those who are sent her! How often I wanted to gather your children together, as a hen gathers her chicks under her wings, but you were not willing." Matt 23:37 NKJV

We spent a couple of hours there in the garden and had a tour of the museum. It was so hot as we walked back to the vans, picked up our lunches and went to the Garden Tomb to eat around 3.45pm. We had a tour there and Holy Communion which was very special. From there we went to the Mount of Olives, walked down to Gethsemane back to the vans and out of the city to a park where Yaron had prepared a wonderful picnic meal for us around 6.45pm. After a good rest there, we travelled to the kibbutzim to spend the night camping. It was a beautiful tranquil place in the countryside, the moon as bright as ever. I didn't sleep much, well no one did really! We could hear the jackals.

Back to Jerusalem the next day, to do outreach two by two instead of as a group, minus the tee shirts! Chris and I had some great conversations, gave out several books and we spent a long time with a man who said he is an atheist, he bought us some carrot juice, he took the book and we prayed for him and others too. It was more productive today – the same street as yesterday. We spent some time with soldiers in the park, had lunch and headed back to Jaffa. I was so tired. We're off to the Galilee tomorrow for two nights – more camping!

The next three days were impossible to recall, no time for journal writing. On the way to the Galilee, we stopped in Haifa, a beautiful port city with much history, Acco (Ptolemais in Acts 21:7) in the distance and then on to Mount Carmel with the story of God's power through Elijah, destroying the prophets of Baal. It reminded me of my first visit there in 2012 and my legs tingling as we sang "These are the days of Elijah". It overlooks the Jezreel valley, Jezreel means God's planting, very fertile, greatly cultivated and goes towards Megiddo. We stopped to speak to a group of soldiers in a wooded area to encourage and thank them for what they do, gave them a hug and some took the book.

It was incredibly hot and when we arrived in Kiryat Sh'mona we went to the river to be refreshed, it was wonderful. Some of the congregation came to have a meal with us and a time of worship and fellowship. Chris, Josephina and I were in one room, and the guys were all over the place, sleeping in the hallway as well, a bit like sardines.

I wrote in my blog: *Yesterday was a really bad day for me, my back was painful and I was so tired. We spent three hours kayaking down the river, an experience I have no desire to repeat though it was funny, getting soaking wet from other people's paddles. Israel got the short straw as he came with us, I was definitely the liability person. There was no way I could have taken a turn to paddle, Philipe and Chris did most of the work and we spent more time going round in circles than down the river, Israel having to get into the water every time we got stuck on the bank among the overhanging branches. It was very shallow but there were one or two small rapids to negotiate so I was hanging on to the ropes. It was so hot and the journey was 8kms. One of our groups thought they were in a race with us but eventually they got caught up with some other dinghies and we arrived before them."*

After lunch and rest time, we went to a kibbutzim to do outreach and I struggled with the heat. However, we had a great conversation with one young woman Mayan, very open, who allowed us to pray for her and she took the book. On to the kibbutzim, we had a bbq, a worship time and by 10pm we were all in bed, mattresses under the moon and stars, seeing exactly what Jesus saw when He was with His disciples. It was amazing. Thankfully, Israel gave me some pain killers and I slept well. For the second time this week, we could hear gunfire and explosions over the border in Syria which is only a few kilometres away.

Home the next day after more outreach in another kibbutzim, unpack, shower and off to the hotel for our Shabbat meal and worship that was amazing. Scott's message very powerful. *"I began to have absolute understanding why I had never been on campaign before!"* The next day being Shabbat, it was quiet, no devotions and I could have a lie in.

We had some reflective worship in the morning and some of my fellow campaigners shared an experience; I could feel the emotion rising and as I began to write in my journal later, the floodgates opened and I'm not sure why. Sunday evening 26 June, was our last meal together for the campaigners, a real feast prepared by Yaron, Chris my room- mate was leaving very early the next morning. We all had to do something to share with everyone afterwards, Andreas and Hansruidi sang a Swiss song with some yodelling, Colin and Phillipe and Lynn and Gerard were so funny, the former singing about each one of us to the tune of Old Macdonald had a farm, the latter doing a sketch of Geraldine alias Gerard as a synchronised swimmer popping up and down from behind the curtain with Lynn's bikini on! Felicitas a young German woman played her violin, what talent she had. Chris and I sang "Rejoice in the Lord always and again I say rejoice", most knew it and then we sang it as a round. As Israel and Marti gave out our certificates I began to cry and could only say "I love you all very much" by which time I was sobbing. I knew at that moment that I would not be going back to Israel, but I didn't know why until a month after I was home.

Two days later, Philipe and Hansruidi left and by the end of the week, those of us who had done life together the previous two weeks would have left except for Andreas. Our devotions with Ziv were wonderful; he began by asking each of us to complete the sentence "God is good because...". For me it was because God had transformed my life from out of the pit and brought me to a place I could never have imagined. When he asked me to read Psalm 40: 1-6 I could feel the emotion rising and struggled to read verse 2, *"He also brought me up out of a horrible pit"*. The very word I had used which touched me deeply.

My last evening in Yafo House was lovely. A young woman from Germany came to visit and Colin got out the guitar when he came home, so the two of them played for Alex and I to have a worship time with them.

I wrote in my journal that it was 35C as I left Tel Aviv for my journey home and I spent most of the time gazing out of the window. It was so wonderful to be up above the clouds as the sun set with a band of bright orange, fading into yellow on the horizon, such beauty with some clouds looking like candy floss, others appearing as snow capped mountains or ice fields. As the darkness descended I could see clusters of lights here and there showing communities dotted along the landscape. It was good to see Melanie and we had a good journey home. My outreach days in Israel now over.

A new journey of Obedience

Three days later I was on my way to the Police Conference for three days with the lead Chaplain and a week after that the Further Education Conference for chaplains. I had been a volunteer chaplain at Grantham College for five years at that point and for Lincolnshire Police Force in Grantham for just over a year. This meant that I had not had any time to reflect on my time in Israel, but when I received a communication from Israel and Marti, then I understood why I would not be going back again. They were leaving the house in Jaffa and going north to Kiryat Sh'mona to begin a new ministry there. Israel was to study for a Theology Degree.

It was so lovely to be back in the prison for the monthly Tuesday evening worship I led for Prison Fellowship, with lots to share with the men. They wanted to know if I knew they had been praying for me every day I was away. I knew for sure that God had kept me safe throughout my time there. These were amazing Christian men who I had come to love and it was always humbling to know they prayed for me as I thought I went there to support, encourage and pray for them.

Within four months of being home, I found myself on the first of four training days for a Kairos Mission[10] to another prison. How did that happen, I asked myself? Whilst I was away someone went to my church and asked my Pastor Jonas if there was anyone who he thought might be interested, to which he replied we do have someone already involved in prison ministry, but because of holidays, I didn't get to hear about it until September. Roger contacted me and shared what Kairos was about, as I had never heard of it before. Kairos is a Greek word meaning "God's special time or the right time". It's a weeklong mission from Monday afternoon until Friday afternoon and men choose to sign up for it. He gave me the regional co-ordinator's name to contact and after two or three long conversations with Richard, he invited me to go to the training in Peterborough. This I think was partly because I was security cleared and he soon understood my passion for prison ministry. It would have been difficult for clearance to be obtained in less than six

---

[10] Kairos UK www.kairosprisonministry.org.uk

months, the mission was scheduled for the last week in March. I couldn't attend the envisioning day but I was available for the training days and could make myself available for the actual week. The training days are an opportunity for team members to get to know one another, to listen to some of the talks and discuss topics in the Team Devotional Guide, worship and eat together too.

I had absolutely no idea what the training entailed but I couldn't believe it when I got there and I found myself in a room with 24 other people whose passion was also for prison ministry. What a lot I had to learn and I was so excited. I didn't seek it, it sought me, God's hand upon the whole journey. This programme began in America and has roots in the Cursillo movement. It is set up slightly differently in the UK but the essence is the same.

Listen, listen, love, love. This is the theme of every Kairos. It reminds us that Kairos is not about preaching or convincing, but we sacrifice our need to be in control and listen with our hearts. The mission is usually centred on the table families named Matthew, Mark, Luke and John, but as this was the first mission in this particular prison, 18 men enrolled and 16 came.

There are usually 24 team members. Each family has a table leader and two assistants, there are observing leaders, two people assigned to the prayer room to pray for those before and after giving a talk, some team members will do the meditations. Last, but not least, there are table servants, of whom I was one.

Team members come from a wide area in the country and for those farthest away, accommodation was provided in the area by Christian families. The days are so long and tiring although exhilarating. We met at 6.30am each morning for breakfast in a church hall, followed by prayer and then followed one another in convoy to the prison. It takes time to get through security and we were in the prison from 8am until about 7pm. The guys left at 6pm and then we had a debrief before leaving.

Included in the programme for the week as expressions of agape love were the place mats which had been made by children in different churches as well as a school and laminated. There were posters to go on the walls with scripture verses of encouragement and wonderful artwork done by creative people in churches as well as prayer chains around the chapel and cookies with every break, 14,000 in all. Not only for the men on the mission, but for every other resident and prison officers a bag of eight home made chocolate chip, oatmeal or ginger cookies. It's a great undertaking and when the men knew that they had come from people from churches over a wide area who have prayed whilst making them, they were shocked. By the end of the week everyone in the prison knew there was something going on in the chapel!

The other important element to the week, is a personal letter written to every man with words of encouragement and scripture, meaning each of the team had to write individual letters, no two to be the same.

The talks are wide ranging, beginning with Know Yourself, I Chose You, Prodigal Son, Choices, You are not Alone, Friendship with God, Acceptance of Self, The Church, Opening the Door, Accepting God's Forgiveness, Forgiveness of Others Part 1, Discovery through Study, Christian Action, The Wall, Forgiveness of Others Part 2, Meditation to Heal Past Memories, The Rooster Story, Obstacles to Accepting God's Grace, Hang in There, Leader's Final Speech and Selection of Family Representatives for Closing, and the Cross Ceremony where every participant is given a Kairos cross.

From the talks given each day, the men discuss their thoughts about what they listened to and would express these in words and pictures on flip chart paper. Later, they would go to the front, say which family they were in and explain it. These would also be put up on the walls. There are talks about forgiveness and there was a service of forgiveness on the Thursday evening. Everyone, including the team, were given slips of rice paper on which to write the name(s) of those they were able to forgive. These were put into bowls of water on the altar, stirred and dissolved. The chaplains prayed for everyone individually and all left the chapel in respectful silence.

As I looked through my journal from the week, I was completely overwhelmed and there were many tears. One of the challenges for me was that I was awaiting a hip replacement and the pain was so severe, but thanks to the team praying fervently for me every day, plus painkillers, I got through the week. At the end of the second day I wrote in my journal: *"What whirlwind days. It was wonderful to meet the guys and how open they were in sharing about themselves so soon after meeting with us. They were so surprised that we were going to eat with them, serve them tea and coffee as well as the cookies."* The whole idea was for them to be part of a family for the week, to be loved, to know they are not alone, LOVE is the heart of Kairos, Christ's love for all of us. Christ calls us to be servants and this required that we give up our control. A servant is at the beckoned call of their Master. We must sacrifice our self-focus to truly be His servant. There can be no division in the team we are united in Christ, however different we all are as individuals. There are times of worship throughout each day.

We go in on Monday afternoon as strangers and leave as friends on Friday, some giving their lives to Christ at the celebration service. It is a really emotional time.

I had the privilege of being part of the team for Kairos II 2018 on the prayer team and Kairos III 2019 as a table leader. Both were incredible experiences I will never forget.

The following comments were written by three of the men on Friday:

"If I'd been asked on Monday by 'trip advisor' to rate the prison as a 'nice place to stay' I would have given it just one star. Today at the end of the course I would give it 10 stars. This course has really helped me. I have loved it."

"I feel I was enrolled on Kairos by God. I had much on my mind when I came, much guilt and much sadness. I have never had a family ever. And yet in Kairos I found a family, I found a feeling of belonging. I prayed for forgiveness with the group and had a strange experience. I went warm from my head to my toes. I believe that was the Holy Spirit and I thank God for putting me on this journey."

"This has been a most amazing course. I want to say it has been an absolute pleasure to be with you people – a team with no agenda just love. I am not changed yet, but I know I am on the right path."

This is what he had written at the beginning of the week:

"When I came to Kairos I was very cynical. I thought this was another programme out to change me with my temper and my bitterness. I done so many in my time...... I was not in a good mood. That night after hearing that talk of the Prodigal Son I went back to my cell and a miracle happened. After months of fretting about my family I found a letter under my door. It was from my family and told me the long-awaited reconciliation had occurred in my family. I saw it as a sign and realised that God had not forgotten me and that the prayer for reconciliation has been answered."

And a poem written by another: "The Lord is my Saviour"

"The Lord is my Saviour I want the world to see,
I once led a troubled life then Jesus rescued me.
It's taken me time to accept this path,
but I continue to walk whilst others laugh.
I used to laugh when stuck in the past,
now I talk to the Lord and have such a blast.
Those lost ones who laugh, what they don't know is
that accepting Jesus makes the heart grow.
The Lord is my Saviour even in such place, yeah I'm in
prison but have a smile on my face. My chains have
been broken, now I speak of God's grace.
People say you're back again,
I say God works in mysterious ways.
I'll use my time wisely to strengthen our bond,
By praising you Lord and singing your songs."

What next?

This is 2020, the year the world has ground to a halt due to the Covid-19 pandemic. My prison ministry is on hold, also chaplaincy at the Police station and street pastors no longer out on Saturday evenings. None of us have any idea when volunteers will be able to return. It's been challenging living on my own but I'm sure no worse than for millions of others living alone. Someone was assigned to me from church to keep in contact with me once a week and a number of people did shopping for me in the early weeks until I could get my own. Several times Jonas called and prayed for me too.

I shed many tears as I began to experience the great loss of not going into the prison, where my heart is and for all that I had the privilege of being involved in, not only the chaplaincy for Prison Fellowship but also from August 2019 until what should have been the end of March, I was running a session on one of the wings once a week for AGE UK, for men with dementia. Some of the activities were to help with their cognitive processes, some just for fun and it was lovely to see them laughing and singing. A moment of light, in what was often a dark time for them. This was a secular group and I didn't know them prior to August, but even those who didn't come to the sessions, would chat to me every week and I was able to ask how they were doing. It is such a privilege to listen to another person share their concerns about life. Some were happy for me to pray with them. The officers were always helpful and I had a resident as an orderly to help me with technology as well as making the coffee.

However, like so many others I painted the shed, weeded the garden and even did some Spring cleaning as well as sorting out the bookshelves, finding books I have since read again. As I began to find a rhythm to my day, including a walk, much more time to read and to pray, it became a very rich time, listening to what God may have to say to me.

In spite of all that God has done in my life, He began to show me that there were things I needed to "change or accept". That's always been difficult for me.

An experience that brought me great anguish came from my devotional reading about Abraham being asked by God to sacrifice Isaac's life. The note writer asked the question: *"If you were instructed by God to* *sacrifice something you consider precious and important, a relationship, an activity or even **a ministry** that you offer in service to the Lord, would you, like Abraham be prepared to lay it down in humble obedience?"*[11]

It's a Friday morning I will never forget. I felt like I had been hit by a train! I wrestled and wrestled, I cried and cried. Several hours later, I said yes Lord, I will give up my ministry if you ask me. Am I at peace about it, not really but God is my life, God gives and God takes away and still I will say blessed be the name of the Lord. If it becomes a reality perhaps the blessing in it all will have been the lockdown.

Late, on another evening, a friend had sent me an ecard out of the blue, I've no idea why I felt the need to open it then, but the message she sent was so beautiful. She said *"praying that you will seek refuge and comfort under God's feathers. I thank God that I can call you my friend. You are such a faithful servant of God and have such a beautiful heart. I pray you will sense His presence and know His all encompassing peace day and night, especially when you are missing all your normal activities and loved ones. I pray this will be a season of refreshing and renewal for you. Sending you lots of love and hugs. Maureen x".*

When I got to bed, the words that came out of my mouth were *"I love the person I have become and am*

---

[11] Encounter with God Daily Devotionals Scripture Union www.scriptureunion.org.uk

becoming". That was the first time in my life I've been able to say I love myself, finally believing God really does love me and I am worth something. That's always been difficult for me, despite all the healing and release from the past.

Now I can sing and **believe** the words from the song: "Who the Son sets free is free indeed"

Who am I that the highest King
would welcome me?
I was lost but He brought me in
Oh His love for me
Oh His love for me

Free at last He has ransomed me,
His grace runs deep.
While I was a slave to sin,
Jesus died for me.
Yes, He died for me.

In my Father's house
there's a place for me
I'm a child of God
Yes I am

I am chosen
Not forsaken
I am who You say I am
You are for me
Not against me
I am who You say I am
Hillsong Worship

Over these months, I have also become aware that the additional time I spend in prayer is so precious and more important now; it is something I must continue even when, God willing, I may be 'doing' rather than 'being'. This may mean I will have to get up earlier in the day and as a night person, it will be a challenge. I've read a number of books and am always hungry to learn more of God and His Ways.

I continue to be in awe of what God brings into my life. Our church ran a 'jacket potato day' 10 years ago once a week in the local Sure Start Centre and also Cherish, a neck & shoulder and hand & arm massage, once a month for women in this community. Many of them were young, single mums and I built up a relationship with Tash. 2014 was the last time I saw her with a new baby and somehow we lost contact. Imagine my shock at receiving a message from her in mid-September. She called me the next day and we had a long conversation, she telling me what a difference I had made in her life. I had no idea at all. She and her husband now live in Scotland and she said that her two older children remember me. What an awesome God we serve.

Love, so amazing so divine,
demands my soul,
my life,
my all

Isaac Watts 1674-1748

APPENDIX 1

AN EXTRACT FROM A MESSAGE TAKEN TO THE SALVATION ARMY

Experiences of worshipping in the different churches for some months from October 2005 and how it has led me to think more deeply about worship and what I've learned from those experiences.

There was a sense on occasion of being a nomad, of no fixed abode, but it was such a liberating experience and I learned so much about meeting with God and God meeting with me in whatever setting and with whatever kind of liturgy. Since we are pilgrims on a journey to God perhaps there is something to learn from engaging in such a nomadic experience for all of us. It has certainly been a very rich experience for me and brought me closer to God through the worship.

It's not the easiest thing to go to a different church week by week, wondering how I might be received, would I know anyone, would anyone speak to me, would I be asked to move because I had chosen to sit in someone else's seat? Silly isn't it, but nonetheless a reality sometimes. I was amazed at how I was made welcome, everywhere I went, no questions asked, no suspicious glances. Just a genuine care for me as a person, something I had not had for a very long time.

From the majesty of the Central Methodist Church to the simplicity of the United Reformed Church, the stained glass windows of St Wulfram's and the glorious sound of the bells, from the grand liturgy of the Eucharist to the simple breaking of bread in the Christian Fellowship, through all of these things I was able to soak up the atmosphere of prayer and peace that pervaded all these places of worship and to know that God was there.

Receiving the bread offered on the plate was real feeding both physical and spiritual and sharing the cup together as a sign of unity in Christ was wonderful and I was struck, perhaps for the first time, that I am used to going to the Lord's table to receive but in some churches the sacraments are brought to us and I found myself thanking God for honouring us in such a way, so much more than we deserve.

I know how important worship through music is to many people and I find this way of worshipping so meaningful for myself. There is such beautiful poetry in many hymns, psalms and songs. Words that touch you somewhere deep inside, fill you with joy or bring you to tears and an experience of the closeness of God. Sometimes there has been more emphasis on the Word or the prayers but all of it taken together is worship. What are the problems we have with worship? Paul tells us that the church in Corinth had difficulties with worship. The problem wasn't what they did so much, but that they had forgotten **who** was at the centre. It's more important to focus on what honours and brings glory to God than whether or not we have got it right or even if we enjoyed it.

Worship is about giving worth to God, it's our response to Him for his love freely given to us, it's what we're made for, worship is about the whole of life. The word worship is mentioned 15 times throughout my NKJ Study Bible, the first tells us about worship as far back as Genesis Ch 22 v5 when Abraham was going up the mountain with Isaac to offer him to God, he tells the young men to wait for him to come back and says *"the lad and I will go yonder and worship"*, Psalm 45:11 *"Because he is your Lord, worship Him* and 95:6 *"come let us worship and bow down, let us kneel before the Lord our Maker*, and so on through the Gospels and to Revelation 4:10 and 14:7. We know very well Psalm 8 showing the smallness of our humanity and the greatness of God in Creation, *"what is man that you are mindful of him, that you have made him a little lower than the angels, that you crown us with glory and honour."* How can we do less than worship and adore such a God as this? If our worship doesn't glorify God, it isn't the work of the Spirit.

It seems strange that the church gets such bad press in light of who God is and what He has done. But is the bad press we get of our own doing? Do we worship in either archaic language or self-indulgent celebration that visitors would find confusing? Perhaps we need to communicate to others in a way that makes sense to them. God is in the business of building His church *that's us*. We must always be drawn back to the centrality of Jesus Christ, He is the author of our salvation and the object of our worship. If we make Jesus that focus then when we go out into the ordinariness of our daily lives perhaps others will see a glimpse of Him in us. As we come together let's sing our praises and then let's go out and worship God in the world with lives that show His love and His power. I love Matt Redman's music, he's a very prolific writer today along with Graham Kendrick and many others. I think his song "When the music fades" sums it up for me.

"I'm coming back to the heart of worship
And it's all about you, all about you Jesus.
I'm sorry Lord for the thing I've made it.
When it's all about you, all about you Jesus."

May we never forget that it's all about Jesus. Amen

APPENDIX 2

WHY SHOULD WE BE GOING INTO PRISONS?

Many would say that we shouldn't be, after all those in prison have committed a crime of one sort or another against another human being or an institution which may have resulted in long term trauma or loss of life. They need to be put beyond the reach of society as a punishment. Should they not have their freedom restricted and be forced to reflect upon the consequences of their actions?

Of course, this is true and I would not want to minimise or dismiss the pain and anger felt by victims of crime. Forgiving those who have violated us in any way is difficult and requires a conscious act on our part. As Christians we are called to love the sinner not the sin, to love the unlovable, to reach the unreachable, much easier said than done, but if we look at what scripture has to say then perhaps we can begin to understand and be encouraged.

Jesus tells us in Matthew's Gospel (Chapter 25: 31-46) that whatever we do for the hungry, the stranger, the naked, the sick and the prisoner we do for Him. The person we visit who is sick or in prison becomes as Jesus to us. How may we know our Lord? We know Him in doing His works, in putting our arms around those who are desperate or alone, in visiting the sick and the prisoners.

We can give to others in a real and tangible way but the focus of our faith and what we do is to be on Jesus. He is God - He is our source. Social concern cannot biblically be divorced from the Christian walk. Jesus equates our treatment of others with our treatment of Himself. What we do for them, we do for Him. I believe that our Christian walk must be related to the service of humanity, not merely a spiritual enterprise important though our spirituality is. When we fail to care for others, we fail to place proper value on them as children of God made in His image just as we are.

Prisoners are still human beings, they have feelings, they have many unmet needs, perhaps as some of us do and if we can share the love of Jesus with them in a non-judgemental way as part of the chaplaincy team, then perhaps in some small way they may feel valued as individuals and with prayer and practical support be enabled to work towards being rehabilitated and able to function successfully in society. I fully understand that some may never be rehabilitated but nevertheless this should not stop us from showing and sharing the love and peace of God which truly *"surpasses all understanding"* as Paul wrote in his letter to the Philippians (Chapter 4 v7)

It is so important to pray for Prisons to be places where justice and fairness is carried out within the system, to pray for the management structures, the chaplaincy teams working under difficult conditions to support prisoners with practical needs and the spiritual dimension in their lives. Many prisoners do come to have a living faith through a personal relationship with Jesus – one man shared with us that if he hadn't been sent to prison, he would not have found Jesus and he was so grateful that his life had been completely transformed.

"And the king will answer them, Truly, I tell you, just as you did it to one of the least of these who are members of my family, you did it to me".

LAST PAGE

If you have been inspired by my story but you are not a Christian, and you would like to explore what it is to know God personally then may I suggest the following:

To begin a relationship with God, you must put your life in His hands.

God is not so concerned with your words as He is with the attitude of your heart.

Each of us must respond by asking Jesus to come into our lives. Then we can know God personally and experience His love and forgiveness.

Prayer is simply talking to God and here is a suggested prayer:

Lord Jesus, I want to know you personally.
I'm sorry for going my own way instead of your way.
Thank you for dying on the cross to forgive my sin.
Please come and take first place in my life and
Make me the person you want me to be.

Could you say this to God and mean it?

Romans 10:13 "For everyone who calls on the name of the Lord, will be saved.

Jesus comes into your life by the Holy Spirit and He will never leave you

All your sins have been forgiven

You have become a child of God. He is your heavenly Father

God has given you a new life and new power to enable you to live a transformed life

You have begun a friendship with God that will last forever and for which God made you

Find a pastor and other Bible believing Christians who can support and help disciple you

Lightning Source UK Ltd.
Milton Keynes UK
UKHW020816061121
393451UK00009B/116